Empty Nesters

...Lose the Guilt

Diane Stolz

2nd Edition

Dedication

To my husband Tom and my kids Bryan, Jeffrey and Julie. Without all of you these stories and this book would not be possible.

Your loving wife and mom

Acknowledgements

To my husband Tom Stolz, who provided technical support throughout this publishing journey and, more importantly, emotional support. To our first-born Bryan Stolz, the editor, who dedicated many hours to combing through my words, correcting and offering insightful suggestions. Sorry but I can't *lose the ellipsis*.... To our middle child Jeffrey Stolz, who creatively did the cover design and formatting for the book. Sorry you had to kick me out of the room that day. And to our youngest, Julie Stolz, who will take on the challenge of publicist to promote the book. I do believe she and Daniel F. have me headed to Facebook. There was also Sarah Stolz, my daughter-in-law, who encouraged us all with her enthusiasm.

I cannot thank all of you enough.

Contents

Introduction

Empty Nesters...*Lose the Guilt*! is a humorous romp through the years of raising kids to remind this "kid pleaser" generation of Empty Nesters why it's finally time to make life about *you*. We'll start by revisiting those moments of parenting that have faded to a blur. Remembering all the day-to-day undertakings of raising the kids, will help you realize, as an Empty Nester, why it's now time for life to evolve around *you*. For our generation of kid-pleaser parents, this is hard. Previous generations parented on the loving premise of like it or lump it or children should be seen but not heard. *They* didn't need this book.

But this generation has delved so deeply into the kids' interests and activities, we arrive at this point in our lives hesitant to embrace all it has to offer, even *guilty* we aren't including our children. *Guilt* unimaginable, after all we've done for those kids! We simply have to find a way to

Lose the Guilt!

Remember back when we felt like a life support system, when every move our children made was dependent on our planning, developing, and execution? How about all those chores charts, the hours of sitting in bleachers, teachers' gifts, and joining the parent-teacher association. There was the hoopla of the holidays, vacation bonding, madness of birthday parties, and shopping meltdowns. Don't forget all the playdates and being talked into getting the mutt, which *was* optional.

You'll soon appreciate all you deserve as an Empty Nester. Besides, our enjoying this time of our lives transforms into our kids' freedom. Until they boomerang back. So, join me as we embark on this humorous walk through the years, remembering why it's now time to enjoy the well-deserved rewards awaiting!

And do it....

amazingly Guiltless!

Chapter One
Life Support System

So about Lamaze...you must be kidding.

Breathe away the pain, not happening. Regardless, the end result is a wonderful bundle of joy snug in our arms. Okay, good, they're taking the baby to do what they do. We're now in the midst of the post-birth hustle bustle, which seems like white noise in the background. "Wow," we say to ourselves, "I did it. I really did it." The time will be embedded in our memories forever: 4:59 p.m., 12:39 p.m., 8:59 a.m. respectively for our kids. Most of us can spout the exact time we gave birth without a thought. We remember those precise times simply because it is at that very moment it all begins.

The hospital stay feels safe. There's always someone to help. Part-time mommy, part-time patient, and always safe. Then, what feels like ten minutes after we deliver, we're out the door and home. *Why didn't I ask more questions when I was in the hospital?* "Are there any written instructions in the patient-belongings bag?" we frantically ask our husbands? The husband, who's standing there staring with a look of, *But you're a woman, don't you automatically know what to do?* It's at that very moment you realize maternal instinct is about as helpful as Lamaze.

The next year of life is like nothing we could have ever imagined. Some senses became heightened, like the sense of hearing. Was that *thud* his bottle hitting the floor from the swing while watching *Sesame Street,* as we're in the next room emptying the dishwasher and talking on the phone? Other senses were dulled, like smell and touch. Think about it. Before you became a parent, do you ever remember touching human urine and feces six to eight times a day? You health care professionals don't count...you wear gloves. Diaper changes become as unconscious an act as buttering toast.

Those eyes in the back of her head your mom talked about? They're real, and now we've got them. You even start to develop a craving for plain Cheerios and Goldfish, whether scooped from the box or the seat of the car. This transformation of the five senses should not be taken lightly. The fibers of our being are changing forever. There is no going back and no controlling its course, not even with Lamaze. This is the first true sacrifice of parenting. Handing over our very own five senses to our children, causing those senses to take on a life of their own...forever.

Soon, we began to experience the delight of the first smile. A baby's grin is the main reason we forgive them for the first year of their lives. It doesn't take children very long at all to realize the impact their smiles have on us. They must notice the sheer outrageous enthusiasm we all show for them. Firstborn children have hundreds of pictures documenting these happy expressions. Second born and on, not so many, but this is when all our children reel us in. In other words, we are completely transformed into their *life support system.*

Becoming their life support system is the

single most unappreciated thing we do as parents. It's not the kids' appreciation I'm talking about here, although they definitely don't appreciate it, it's all the other aspects of our lives. Take the first doctor appointment when our child was two weeks old. Much like a mother bear, the protective instinct kicked right in. We drove a little slower, held the wheel a little tighter, and any car coming close to cutting you off felt like an attack on our baby cub. Even the doctor approaching with the obnoxiously large tongue blade felt threatening. So when we stood in the way to keep one comforting hand on our child, resulting in the doctor having to climb over us, they should have understood. When we grabbed the nurse's hand at our child's first immunization, pleading for another minute, they needed to understand. When we stumbled out of the office disoriented, dripping perspiration, and forgetting to write the check for the co-pay, they needed to understand. But they didn't. Nope, instead they talked about us in the staff lounge over coffee.

Another example was at the elementary school. Man oh man, no understanding there at all. We arrived on the first day of kindergarten, showered and dressed as if going to a job interview, entrusting our child, also perfectly groomed, to the school to educate. Handing over to them the responsibility of their breathing, talking, walking, sitting, eating and, if they'll do it in school, excreting. Everything we completely wrapped our life around for what seemed like thirty or forty years, but was usually only four or five. And all we do is ask a few little questions about the sturdiness of the chains on the swings in the playground, wonder aloud if three kids in one seat on the bus is a good idea, and express our concern about the teacher wearing the top with her cleavage showing. Again, they needed to understand. But they didn't. Nope, instead they talked about us in the teachers' lounge over ham sandwiches and tomato soup.

Shopping was another challenge that showed the outside world's total lack of understanding of a parent's life support system role. A single item you wanted to find so badly for your child became the whole focus of your existence. You spent more money on gas during your search than the item was even worth.

You elbowed your way through racks and tables to find the size or exact color you wanted. You nicely asked the salesperson, "Do you have a size large Steelers jersey in the back?" or "Do you possibly have this Barbie backpack in purple?" When they nonchalantly replied, "I don't think so," you just couldn't help yourself. Out it came in a harsh, threatening voice. "Could YOU CHECK?" Yup, you yelled at them, and they really did need to understand. But they didn't. Nope, instead they went to the back, pretended to look for thirty seconds, returned to tell you no then talked about you at the water cooler during their break.

They did not understand.

So it's obvious how underappreciated being a child's life support system is. But let's not forget the tremendous amount of endurance it also entailed. In the first eighteen years of our child's life, an hour rarely went by when we didn't need to check on, get, or do something for them. Basically, our lives were a constant hum of checking, getting, and doing. They come into this world completely helpless, and it's a very gradual process to their becoming "independent human beings." We deserve credit for just enduring it. The process involved our children having to conquer many milestones along the way. Those monumental moments that tested us, as well as thrilled us, were usually documented in a picture now stuffed in a box at the back of our closet.

One of our children's first milestones was crawling. This seemed to happen before our eyes with very little effort on our part. You're in the kitchen making dinner, the baby is playing on the floor next to you, you look away, you look back, and they're gone. They crawled! That pretty much sums up crawling except for the need to constantly survey the baby's surroundings. This is when a split second took on a whole new meaning. *Wow, she was beside me and now she's on the other side of the house.*

Tupperware cabinets became hiding places, lint on the floor became snacks, and up went the gate blocking the stairs. Unless you were a high jumper at some point in your life or a Rockette, those gates were not easy to manage.

Milestone number two is walking...usually. Sometimes girls talk before they walk. Face it, ladies. We get our priorities straight right out of the gate.

Walking is especially exciting for parents of babies with reflux. Reflux is babies spitting up a sour-smelling gooey material every five minutes that the doctor assures you is normal. Our firstborn had projectile reflux. He could shoot out three feet and, if his head had spun around, he could have starred in *The Exorcist*. Parents of a child with reflux know, thanks to gravity, when they walk, it stops. Walking is also exciting for the babysitter, usually the person privileged to see our children take their first step. Yup, even if we've never left our child with a sitter before, the kid would walk during the one hour we did. I consider this a child's first crack at tormenting their parents. This new achievement forced us to place Christmas trees inside playpens, move breakables to higher shelves, install childproof cabinet latches that even we couldn't open, and cover our refrigerator with educational magnets. Who among us doesn't occasionally come across a letter magnet amongst the cheese spreaders in a kitchen drawer?

Next was the talking milestone. This one starts out great because it replaces the point and grunt. Finally the game of charades is over and our child can actually tell us what they want. We love this until we realize their asking us what they want becomes the main focus of their conversation throughout the rest of their childhood, teens, and early twenties. Okay, I'm exaggerating, there's also *no*. The times they are not asking us what they want, they're telling us *no*. We quickly realize any effort we put into encouraging them to voice their needs and share their opinions has backfired. We long for a quiet moment. Then, one day, we get one. Yup, we get a quiet moment, and...we panic.

Where are they? What's wrong? Are they sick?

Did I miss an immunization? We then realize the hum of their voices, as exhausting as it may be, is actually reassuring.

Even when they move out, we need to hear their voices to reassure ourselves they are doing okay. We make the phone call pretending we forgot to tell them something.

We do our parental instinctive assessment. If we detect any sort of dismay, we spend the night tossing and turning. Then we make another phone call the next day pretending we need to tell them something else. We discover they were fine all along and just hung over from being out with their friends. But, somehow we're reassured.

How about one of the more difficult milestones, for us, not them, which is the complicated feeding milestone. First of all, every American child's first solid food is a plain Cheerio. We must have all signed something agreeing to it before leaving the hospital. A plain

Cheerio unless Grandpa slipped them a sour-cream-and-onion potato chip when they were three months old. This happens frequently because grandpas always interpret a baby's gnawing on their fist when teething as hunger. You could not convince them otherwise. You only found out about his sly act after the party was over, two diapers later.

And how about the food pyramids? What a struggle to get our kids to eat all the foods on that thing. Everywhere we looked there were food pyramids hanging on walls pressuring us to get the right foods into our kid. The doctor's office, the dentist, the grocery store, pharmacy, school. I even saw one at the mini-golf snack bar. Now come on. The prompts were so intense if we blew this we were loser parents for sure. Turned out the only way not to blow this was to disguise all healthy foods with Cheez Whiz or ketchup. Eventually, even that stopped working, and the only things they wanted to eat were sour-cream-and-onion potato chips...thanks, Grandpa. At that point we gave up and just bought the gummy vitamins in the shape of Disney characters. Later, we found out those rot their teeth. Moving on.

Then there was the milestone of our kids graduating from a crib into a big-kid bed. An emotionally scarring milestone, again for us more than them. To uncage our children during the night was scary. They were now free to roam around the house and get into things while we slept. Turned out the only thing they really wanted to get into was their parents' beds. Even after we bought the Sesame Street or dancing bear comforter set, they would not stay in their bed. There they stood at the foot of the bed at 2:00 a.m., in their glow-in-the-dark Ghost Buster pajamas, scaring the ever living life out of us. This seemed to go on forever. They showed up, we put them back, they showed up, put them back, up, back, up, back until you were so exhausted you, of course, let them crawl under the covers with you. How can a person standing only thirty-five inches tall monopolize an entire queen-size mattress? It goes against the laws of physics, but they do. Sometimes we tried sitting on the floor outside their room to get them to stay put and fall asleep.

Boy, the stuff I got done on that floor: bills, coupon clipping, a manicure. This, at least, was productive. We did, however, have to be very mindful of floorboards with this plan. One squeak could send us right back to start. Finally, they stay in the bed. Like most milestones, we never really know why it happens. But they do, we're thrilled...done. Not so fast. We still woke up every morning with their nose planted on ours and their squeaky little voice asking "Are you awake? Are you awake?"

Next is the mystifying milestone of our kids' attempts at dressing themselves. Mystifying because this is when kids take their first crack at self-expression, and we're never really sure how it was going to go. It also explains why you see children wearing shorts and tank tops in January and winter boots in July. Also, most kids prefer nakedness the first few years of their lives. We hope by wearing clothes ourselves every day, they will follow our example, but they often prefer to follow the example of a superhero or Disney princess instead. This explains the Power Ranger and Snow White outfits in church. Our son wore Underoos on his head as a helmet an entire summer with a backpack as his power booster. I think red boots were involved, too. One thing is certain, if children locked into wanting to wear something, it was like moving heaven and earth to convince them otherwise. All the usual bribes did not work. This also continued right through the college years. I would actually venture to say it got worse. No longer mystifying, more just mind-boggling. It's when our other son's cargo pants, shredded on the bottom from dragging, became his main wardrobe staple. New stuff looks old, tops too low, hems too high, and.... *What does that shirt say?* They would *not* listen to our reasonable, loving advice.

Okay, how about the potty training milestone? I know, I know. Nothing left its mark on us like potty training. This required clever and consistent interventions on the part of the parent. It was so all-consuming, we barely left the house. A constant vigil for the squirm or grimace indicating they had to go. Let your guard down even once and the results led to no M&M reward from the jar on the toilet tank and no sticker on the chart.

Thinking back, we should have upped the ante on this. With potty training, we were also working against a toddler's very high tolerance for the state of yuckiness. It's hard to wrap your head around a child's lack of regard for existing, unfazed, with a load in his pants. We would worry whether this was normal. It didn't help hearing the parent at playgroup bragging how they potty trained their kid in two hours. To make matters worse, they'd offer advice. In fact, everyone wanted to give advice on how to accomplish this milestone. Our heads were spinning. Did we try the potty-in-front-of-the-TV tactic or the diaperless-roam-about system? The stress got so bad *we* started to eat all the M&Ms from the jar on the toilet tank. Finally, after we were worn down to a fragment of our existence and had gained five pounds, our child started to use the bathroom. After all the charts, stickers, candy, and whatevers, it came down to...they changed their mind.

Let's fast-forward to the most trying milestone of all in the quest of our kids becoming independent human beings...Driving. Unlike other milestones, learning to drive actually was as trying for our kids as it was for us. They had to admit we knew more about something than they did. They had to follow our instructions on driving and parking if they wanted to get through this, as well as, get the keys to the car. If you'd seen our garage door a few years back, you'd understand why I included parking. Making it the parents' job to teach kids how to drive is very cruel. There should be overnight camps for this. Send them away for a week and they come back knowing how to merge onto an interstate and do a three-point turn. But, no, the already weary parents of a sixteen year old are the ones left with the task. Oh, sure, there's drivers' education, but those teachers are no fools, they want the kids to know the basics before they'll take them on. So we were the ones who drove them down to the church parking lot their first time behind the wheel. We were the ones who experienced the terror when they looked at us and said, "Wait...what...that one's the brake?" Didn't their Little Tikes Coupe teach them anything? We were the ones holding our breath hoping they remembered which one is the brake when we finally take them out on the road. And we were the ones sitting beside them when they mix it up, panic, and stopped cold in the middle of the intersection. Oh yes, we were the ones.

Okay, deep breath. That was then and this is now. Our kids have finally reached all of these important milestones of life, and we are no longer their day-to-day life support system. They no longer need us to comfort them at the doctor's, interrogate their teachers, or harass a salesperson for them. For the most part, they are now independent human beings. Problem is we got used to being this person for them, so it's only natural to feel a little slighted. In fact, it feels a little like being fired. In reality, we've been reassigned. We are working on an on-call basis and it's best not to focus too closely on who we've been replaced with. Mainly it's the other eighteen- to twenty-something-year-olds they're now living with who have far more wisdom to offer them than we do. This is, of course, after we've provided them with all the necessities to live with those eighteen- to twenty-year-olds. As completely unjust as this may seem, I will simply ask you to hold that thought. It will help you immensely for the *guiltless* part of this book.

In the end, this is a good thing. Think about it. We now hear after the fact about their antics. There's nothing we can do about it, and they somehow got through it without our help. Hard to believe, but it's true. In fact, our three kids have a five-year statute of limitations on telling us things. Even better! I knew we raised those kids right.

So now that our kids have become independent human beings and we are no longer their life support system, it's time to appreciate the freedom. It's time to reward ourselves for all those years of meeting our children's every want and need.

Even as consuming and exhausting as it all was, we miss it, feel a void. This is the crazy part of parenthood. But it's time to develop the mindset of the void we feel is the payoff. Still hesitant? Let me seal the deal here.

Remember the days when the only way to get a little time to yourself was to pay a babysitter or leave the kids with the in-laws, regardless of the risk? Do you remember having to cut up your kid's food in the shape of sailboats so they would eat, before you could start your own meal...cold?

Remember running from activity to activity, dreaming of what it would be like to come home from work...and stay there?

Okay, then, let's start by appreciating the fewer demands and the sense of calm we now have in our lives. Appreciate how we were a life support system for them for all those years, and wouldn't change that for the world, but the time has come to support our own lives now. To actually think about what *we* might like to do when we get home, and, believe me, the possibilities are endless.

For instance, have you walked through a craft store lately looking at things that might interest you? I know we've been there for school projects, but look with an eye for something you may want to do. You can make or remake anything. Stamp it, paint it, stencil it, stitch it, and frame it. It's all there. I think I even saw a decoupage kit. I haven't done decoupage since Girl Scouts!

Or maybe exploring a new sport would better suit you. Sporting goods stores have many great options, and they provide instructions. Even if sports were never really your thing, these stores make it look so good, you'll want to try one anyway. In fact, my husband and I bought kayaks after a visit to one.

We now love gingerly stepping into a kayak and taking a paddle around a lake on the weekend. Did we see ourselves doing this when we were a life support system? Absolutely not!

Starting to sound good, isn't it? Congratulations, you are now on your way to an Empty Nester *guiltless* existence. Maybe you're realizing just how long you have put your own interests on hold. Maybe you're truly considering taking ownership of this void in your life and actually embracing it. Realizing you can do anything you want, whenever you want, for as long as you want, once you discover, or rediscover, what you want. Whatever it is you decide to embrace in this new existence, please, turn off your cell phone while doing it. Let those eighteen- to twenty-something-year-olds your kids are now living with handle anything that may come up. Because...you happen to be "supporting" *your* life at the moment!

And doing it...

amazingly *Guiltless*!

Chapter Two
Chores/ "Picky-Uppy"

Oh, how we approached chores for our children with unrealistic expectations. We were such authorities as we watched parents around us seemingly blow it over the years. You know, before we had kids, when we thought we knew everything about raising them. "I can't believe they let their kids get away with that," we'd mutter with disgust. "Why don't they make those kids clean it up?" To our naked, childless eyes it all seemed so simple.

Then, suddenly, it was our turn, and we were full of confidence and know-how. Let the games begin. We start by cheerfully saying to our three-year-old, "Come put your blocks away, honey. Time for Picky-Uppy," thinking that would make it sound fun. And our three-year-old looks us square in the eye and proclaims a very loud and clear *no*. We reassured ourselves this was typical behavior for a three-year-old and we should expect it. It's really a matter of setting limits. We then proceeded to spend the next fifteen years attempting to do just that.

Right off the bat, we were at a disadvantage. As the generation of no spanking, we basically had to come up with something that scared a kid as much as spanking to get them to do things. Unfortunately, there isn't any reasonable thing out there to do that, so we had no choice but to go with a psychological approach. Besides, it all seemed so reasonable. You make the mess, you clean the mess. You drop it, you pick it up. There are wooden decorative plaques everywhere proclaiming this. Most of us had taken a course or two in psychology in the past and felt confident we could handle this. Despite the words of wisdom from Grandma and Grandpa weighing in along the way. "Psychological mumbo jumbo," they would say to us, and then go on and on about how they did it in "their day." Of course, how they did it in "their day" would be reportable to Protective Youth Services today.

So we proceeded as suggested by our Psych

101 class with a calm, reasonable explanation for our seemingly reasonable request...*very psychological.* When unsuccessful, our calm, reasonable explanations escalated to a stronger stance, throwing our weight around now, again for a seemingly reasonable request...*still psychological.* And even after mustering up a voice that sounded way too much like our own parents, with still no success, it became apparent our psych course stunk and there's way more to this than meets the naked, childless eye.

One thing was for sure. Consistency in getting our kids to do chores was absolutely imperative and absolutely impossible. Impossible unless we committed to following them around from the time their feet hit the ground in the morning until they were tucked back into bed at night...for fifteen years. As I said, impossible. That's why even occasional consistency on this was a remarkable accomplishment.

We surely all started out consistent, keeping our eyes on the ball and never wavering. But that's when their toys only amounted to a few trucks or dolls and a tent. By the time the children reach age four, we realize our home is overrun with our kids' stuff. Where in the world did it all come from, you wonder. Did the neighbor kids leave some of this? Did I buy all this stuff? Are they shoplifting? There was barely any sign of our own existence left in the house. It's when we got to that overwhelmed point that it happened. Yup, the day that we dropped the ball on getting our kids to do "picky-uppy." That one day that we closed our eyes to the mounds of toys sprawled all over the house and just sent them on to bed, was indeed the game changer. This drop in consistency on our part was the best gift we could have ever given our kids. It was the first time they saw us in a different light, *human*. We will regret that day for many years to come. They figured out that when we're distracted or exhausted, they can get out of stuff. And if they get us to that vulnerable state of mind, which they quickly perfect, they *win*.

Next the panic sets in. "We're raising slobs."

"What are we going to do?" "Our kids have no concept." Sheer panic. You start to wonder if it counts as abuse if the object is thrown, and would a Protective Youth Services referral be worth it if it does. But of course, instead, we all came up with *A Plan*. The plans that parents have come up with over the years to get their kids to do chores could be a book all its own. It's the most talked about issue amongst parents from the toddler years till, well let's just say, until it becomes their roommate or spouses' problem. But until then it's our problem, so out of desperation we made *the chart*. The chart was a plan suggested in many of the parenting books we used to guide us through child rearing. They told us they provide accountability for our kids' weekly chores. Oookay. The chart should be neatly outlined with assigned chores and include a check-off system, hence the accountability part. Oookay. For younger children, it should involve stickers because that's what they really love. For older children, it should involve threats, because that's the only thing they understand. The chart is usually placed on the refrigerator, sometimes color coded, and always ignored after three weeks. Oookay.

After ditching the chart, we often moved on to the *Restricting-an-activity-until-the chore-is-done plan*. I guess we thought this would make more of an impression.

Unfortunately, it ended up having many loopholes.

Loophole #1. We'd say "You are *not* going with us until you do your chore." They'd scream, "Nooo, I don't want to." At that point, the entire family was sitting in the car with the motor running, and you were already forty minutes late for the in-laws. You really had no choice but to negotiate an extension. We'd say, "Ok, you *will* do it when we get home" and they didn't. Don't beat yourself up. No one is expected to have the energy to enforce chores after a visit with the in-laws.

Loophole #2. We'd say, "You *can't* go outside until you put that away." They'd say, "But I still want to play with it," and start playing with it again instead of going outside. We'd say, "Okay, then you *will* put it away when you're done" and they didn't. Don't feel bad. How could you have known they would only play five more minutes then slip out the door without you noticing.

Restrictions could also backfire and end up more of a punishment for us than for our kids. If your child's reaction was a full-blown tantrum, very distressing. If their reaction was the opposite, and they completely ignored your picky-uppy request, even more distressing. If either went on for more than thirty minutes, we cleaned it up ourselves. I'm also pretty sure everyone knows the parent who threw all their children's belongings out the bedroom window, but I'm not sure what plan that falls under.

It only seemed reasonable to try a *bribery plan* next in getting our kids to do chores. The beauty of bribery was there's always something to dangle in front of a child that they *really, really, really* want. Time-sensitive items like melting ice cream bars, favorite TV programs, or a friend peering in the screen door wanting to play worked best. This at least assured you of an accelerated clean-up job. Yes, the illusion of clean. Personally, I was fine with that unless company was coming in the next two weeks. My kids would gladly give you detailed descriptions of my cleaning frenzies when company was coming, but this is not their book.

Eventually, our kids figured out they could turn the bribery plan around and use it on us, another loophole. "If I keep my room clean, can my bedtime move to nine thirty?" or "I'll empty the dishwasher every day if I can watch wrestling on Monday nights." Things we would never in this world think of allowing suddenly seemed okay. In our desperation to get our kids to do chores, we watched our standards gradually crumble. It seemed they were now handling us, something I refer to as "the inmates running the jail." The sooner we bagged the bribery plan, the better.

The only thing left was to pay them. That's right, the *allowance plan*. This ended up the only real way to get a chore out of your kid. An allowance is simply a parent paying their child to do something the child should be doing anyway. Can't believe we all bought into this. Most kids developed a surprisingly sharp memory with this plan.

Not for the chore, of course, but for the allowance. There they'd stand every Saturday morning, beaming, with an outstretched hand "I get my allowance today." As we forked over the cash, our minds were racing *Wait a minute. What was this for again?* Mind still racing *Did they ever do that*? As you desperately try to collect your thoughts, you vaguely remember buying a movie ticket to count as their allowance. Or was it last month? Unless you had statistical evidence, you were screwed. The good news, it was the first glimmer of our child's ability to remember something without our reminding them of it. Yes, we were now grasping at straws.

Even when it was questionable if they deserved this monetary gain, we plodded on, satisfied we could strike a chore off our to-do list. Even better, they would now have some spending money of their own. Responsibility is being taught, pride is being built, all is good in the Land of Oz.

Then spring sports started. Not only was it impossible to get chores done when spring sports started, doing pretty much anything was impossible...unless, of course, Coach okayed it.

The real validation of our failure in getting our kids to do chores was college. In college, kids progressed to an unimaginable level of disarray that went beyond their worst moments of mayhem at home. The boys were the worst. It started in the dorm hallway before even reaching their room. "That smell, what is that smell?" "Why do they throw pizza boxes in the hall?" "Whose shoe and hoodie is laying there?" Stepping over items to reach your son's room, the door opened and there was his roommate in his boxers.

After putting pants on, he politely invited you in to "hang out" while you waited for your son to get out of class. And there it was, the environment your child had been living in, day in and day out, since you dropped him off. As you were trying to calculate the number of beer cans constructing the pyramid in the corner, his roommate proudly reported how they cleaned up last night for your visit.

The girls, on the other hand, greeted you with thirty-five different perfume and hair-product aromas melding in the hallways of their dorms. We should have known better than to trust that illusion of clean. Upon opening their door, you realized, aside from the lack of beer cans, they were not much better.

You're sure you remember packing her a hamper and fear what might be harboring in the carpet her clothes are lying all over. You try to take some pride in the fact she thought to put up curtains, *boys never do that*, but wonder how long the dishes have been sitting in the sink, and was that a dust bunny or a live animal under the bed? Whether it's your daughter or your son, when they went to college you realized the condition of their room at home was only an amateur ranking.

Why then do we clean their room like they're company for visits home? They dump a carload of junk into their picture-perfect bedroom, Yup, that you cleaned. Junk that slowly mutates into an unrecognizable, monstrous pile that eventually creeps out into other parts of the house, yup, that you also cleaned. I know, we want to make their visits home pleasant, but we must remember we have spent half our lives desperately trying to teach them to pick up after themselves, and they still don't. Yet, we still clean like maniacs every time they come home. Honestly, there's something wrong with us.

And even when you put your foot down and tell them they have to leave their room as clean as when they arrived, they know. They know you can't bring yourself to enforce it.

They know you're so glad to have them home you won't want to risk ruining the visit. They also know we'll throw in the towel, which was also left on the floor, and will clean it up all over again when they leave. Yup, they are clearly working the system. So are we going to do something about this? Ummm.... Nope, absolutely not.

Now that our kids are independent human beings and either in a dorm or a real place of their own, everything changes. They have roommates or spouses and in-laws in their lives. We parents will never be able to influence our children like they can. Even though we tried, these are the people who will end up being "the plan" that finally makes our kids do something about their mess. Basically, we really never had a chance in getting our kids to pick it up.

We could beat ourselves up about this frequently unsuccessful part of parenting, but I like to think we were merely victims of circumstance. We couldn't help the time-consuming activities overtaking our lives during the child-rearing years. And, when you think about it, have we really failed? Psychologists are still unable to solve many social issues in the world and end up settling for raising awareness, right? In fact, raising awareness is a really big thing right now. As a society, we don't raise awareness for things we have conquered. No, we raise awareness for things we are working on conquering. I'm not saying we should have T-shirts made screaming out the message of chores awareness. But fifteen years of unsuccessfully hounding our kids, day in and day out, to pick up their junk, should definitely qualify as raising awareness. So, we haven't done so badly after all.

We also shouldn't underestimate the impact this journey will have on our children down the line. Indeed, our desperate tone of voice will echo in the back of their heads for many years to come in their moments of disarray, and our disgruntled faces will flash in front of their eyes. But best of all one day, one glorious day, they will find themselves using our same tone of voice, with *our* same disgruntled look on *their* faces, when trying to get their own kids to "Pick It Up"! And maybe, just maybe, that's reward enough.

Let's also not forget the sense of joy we experience after we clean their room and it stays clean! Even though we're miffed they *again* left it such a mess before heading back to their digs, it's still great. Once we stop tearing up over the picture collage on their mirror, it really is great! Don't you find yourself walking in and out of their room, over and over, enjoying its cleanliness and order? Of course you do, and I'll bet you're feeling guilty about it.

Stop right there. Let's review the title of this book: Empty Nester...*Lose the Guilt!* Okay then, time to remember back when the doorbell rang unexpectedly and we had to dash around in a panic, throwing toys into closets before opening the door. Remember all the organizing systems: the racks, bins, shelves, buckets, margarine containers...we tried everything. They all worked for a few days, or until a neighborhood kid came over. Then it was back to the Barbie shoes mixed in with the Polly Pockets, and the Legos mixed in with the Ninja Turtles. We thought it was hopeless and this would be our life forever. But look where we are now, we have rounded the bend and should be elated! We can walk in and out of their room for days at a time, and the shelves are still tidy. We deserve to be elated over this!

We now need to take a walk through our homes with a new set of eyes. What do we really want it to look like with the Barbie shoes and Legos gone, or at least hidden in a closet? I guarantee you will see things you haven't noticed in years. Wooo...how old is that thing? Didn't you glue it together once? *Get rid of it*! How about that? Didn't you take it from your grandmother's house to be nice?

Out of here! We all have a chipped vase we turn to the wall every time we dust...it's time. *Toss it*! Now for the kids' rooms. I'm not suggesting you get rid of everything, but don't you think it's time to scale down the shrine? Do you really need to keep the plastic snow-cone cup from the 2002 Apple Harvest Festival? I'm sure you can safely ditch the glow-in-the-dark stars hanging from their ceiling. *Gone*!

Next, off to the discount stores. Make a list, and don't forget to measure and bring color samples. Out with the old and weary, in with the new and fresh, the rejuvenated! Soon you'll not only be walking into a picked-up house, but a revitalized house as well.

It's time to look at your home with a new perspective. Gone are all the things you have become so accustomed to seeing you don't notice them anymore. I guarantee the kids won't even notice, or at least not long enough to miss a beat. You deserve to reward yourself after all those years of scratching your head and strategizing with getting your kids to do chores.

It's time to celebrate!

And do it...

amazingly Guiltless!

Chapter Three
School Daze

This starts out feeling like it's just wrong. They're only wearing a size four, have been out of diapers for a year or so, and you're still cutting up their food. Regardless, the state summons us to send our children off to learn how to read. Reluctantly, we get the required physical, buy the latest Disney lunch box, and even a nice new pair of shoes. Then with what seems like a moment's notice, we're dropping them off for their first day of school. This could be the first real feeling of *guilt* we all experience. Yes, after all the kicking and screaming, on our part not the child's, we actually liked this...in fact we loved this!

Wow, three to four hours of free time. Three to four hours! First grade, holy cow, six hours in a row. Even if we had other kids at home or our children went to day care, this was a real game changer. Of course we felt the heart strings tug as we peeled them off our leg into the hands of the patiently waiting teacher. Even if the child trotted off without a glance back, you couldn't help but drop a tear or two. But really, was it anything ten minutes at the mall couldn't cure? Unfortunately, we were not equipped to handle the *guilt* we felt about all this newfound freedom, no not equipped at all. It made us vulnerable prey, and they got us. Yup, we joined the PTA.

Suddenly, we're sitting through meetings promised to be one hour tops, but lasting at least two. We're watching our hand fly impulsively into the air every time we hear the words, "Can I have a volunteer?" Now, instead of enjoying the time our kids were under someone else's care, we were booked to work a fundraiser. Instead of trying all those new recipes we ripped out of the magazines in the pediatrician's waiting room, we're fixing a quick dinner so we can work a book fair. Somehow, providing food, shelter, and clothing for our kids wasn't enough. Even providing multiple extracurricular activities, religious education, yearly physicals, a biannual dental checkup, and birthday parties, while keeping them up on their homework assignments and hygiene needs, was no longer enough. For some reason, we still felt it was necessary to join the PTA. We signed up hoping our child's education would benefit from our presence. Fact is, it didn't matter then, it doesn't matter now and it will *never* matter that you joined the PTA!

There were advantages, however, to being a member of the PTA. Oh yes, it kept you in the know about all the issues the school would rather you not know about. Not necessarily from the actual meeting, but from the conversations afterward. Since PTA parents were in the schools a lot doing their part, they had the dirt on everything. They knew what kid was in the principal's office on a given day, what the teachers ordered for lunch, who was out of dress code, and if the leaking fountain in front of room 112 was fixed. Once I even found out my son was picked to get an English writing award before he heard he was getting it.

Joining the PTA also allowed you to have a

say on important decisions affecting how the school operated. You know, decisions like whether the spaghetti dinner was held in September or April, what symbol went on the front of the school shirt, and what kind of flowers the music teacher received on performance night. These decisions involved more hours of deliberating than Congress requires passing legislation. We took on our causes with a vengeance and left our mark on the history of the school. Even when the cause got voted down the next year by new members, we could still walk away knowing we were members of the PTA and we were in the know.

We also knew, when it came to homework with our kids, timing was everything. Obtaining the optimal blood sugar level in a child during homework held the greatest chance for success. After-school snacks were invented for parents who wanted their kids to do homework before dinner. There was a real advantage to this. When your kid informed you they needed a Styrofoam ball to make a planet for tomorrow, you had time to jump in the car, drive to the store, and get it. On the other hand, anti-anxiety drugs were invented for parents who wanted their kids to do homework after dinner. Those parents had to dig through the attic for their Styrofoam ball.

Helping our kids with their homework was an important responsibility. This was fine until they reached fourth grade. By then it became very clear how much elementary school education had changed since the sixties. *You call that division? What do you mean you don't carry the number anymore! What, no diagramming sentences to find the verb? Are you sure you're allowed to use a calculator for math?* At this point, it was hard for us to help them, and all we could do was reinforce the importance of doing a good job, making sure they put a finished something into their backpack at the end of the night. We crossed our fingers, which *we* used for doing math in the sixties, and hoped for the best.

Of course, once our kids started to use a computer to do homework, everything changed.

They assured us it was fine with their teachers to use the Internet as a resource. They also assured us they were only checking their homework assignments with their friends on instant messenger. We were *invading their privacy* if we peered over their shoulders when they were checking those assignments. They were clearly socializing instead of doing homework, but *we* were invading *their* privacy. The abbreviations they used made it hard to interpret exactly what they were saying, but we still had enough evidence to bust them.

It felt like cheating to me. It seemed too easy. They no longer had to go to a library and use the Dewey Decimal System to find a book on the shelf. Instead they typed a subject into Google and up came all the information they needed. They no longer had to write a sloppy copy and then feel the pressure of writing it neatly on the final draft with no mistakes, especially if it had to be done in ink. Our generation knows all too well those pen erasers never worked. Our kids were even missing the experience of trimming off the frayed edges of a paper after tearing it out of the spiral notebook. These experiences were an integral part of our education and contributed greatly to who we are today. Let's hope the age of technology doesn't backfire on us and our kids end up with marshmallow brains someday. But as far as the computer homework for our kids, we did put our foot down on allowing them to Google *elephant*, hit print, and hand the paper in for their science report.

I feel proud of that.

Getting our kids through science projects alone could be the biggest reason to reward ourselves. Science Projects not only involved parental assistance, they required assistance from the immediate family, extended family, friends, and sometimes your plumber. Mostly because these projects required daily watering, daily measuring, refrigeration, or power tools. This went on for weeks until the collected data was aesthetically attached to a display board, usually frantically accomplished the night before it was due. The grand finale was the delicate maneuver of delivering the project to school. If you remember correctly, these things could not go on the bus. Even when driving at 10 mph, with the poster board secured on all sides, pieces would loosen, parts would crack, and stuff just broke.

Once there, finding a good spot on a display table was most important and could get ugly amid the mad rush of parents scurrying around searching for optimal table placement. It was very important to never get stuck next to the kid whose father was a mechanical engineer with a degree from MIT or a project involving fire. It was always best to slide in next to the laundry-detergent project. In the end, and I'm not at all proud of this, I do admit to begging my kids *not* to do a science project when they became optional. I know, I know, but don't forget...I did join the PTA!

Another big stressor in keeping up with our kids' school demands was teachers' gifts. I learned about this obligation through the PTA. The word out there was this could make or break it for your child. If parents didn't get their act together on teachers' gifts, their child could kiss student of the month, helper of the day, and even line leader good-bye. Now, most of us have worked day in and day out throughout our lives, putting in an honest day's work, and are good at what we do. Have any of us ever received gifts of this nature? On the other hand, did we really want to risk jeopardizing our kids' future? Soooo...we were in! It wasn't too bad when the first child started school. It got a little more challenging with a second. With three or more going, holy cow. There was the Christmas gift, Teacher Recognition Day, and the end-of-year gift. If it only stopped there, but if a child took an instrument, enrichment courses, or visited the school nurse four out of five days a week, there was another whole group of expectant gift recipients. What about the principal? The principal could definitely make or break your child's future. Consistency was an absolute must. Imagine missing someone who was given a gift the year before. Are you kidding me? Scholastic suicide. And imagine giving someone the same gift twice? Yup, accurate record keeping had to be maintained as well. That meant a whole lot of Avon and scented candles to keep track of. If your neck is tensing from remembering it all...understandable.

It all paid off when our child came bounding in the door announcing they received an award for the best essay in the third-grade class. An award! Oh my goodness, a real award. Jumping up and down, trying to decide who to call first, you began changing the dinner menu to their favorite food. You're certain they had proven themselves to be college scholarship material. Harvard, here we come! You anxiously watched them reach into the bottom of their backpack and pull out a crinkled and tattered photocopied certificate with their name misspelled. You immediately rummaged through the mail for the magazine with an article titled *Ten Best Ways to Flatten Wrinkled Paper*. Should you request their social security number on the award to verify identity because of the misspelled name?

Perhaps next month's magazine would have an article about preserving documents. You were too thrilled with their outstanding performance to scold them about keeping their papers disorderly, and thrilled with yourself for going with the photo albums instead of scented candles for teachers' gifts that year. And so began...*The False Road to Full-Ride Scholarships.*

If only we'd known we would have thirty to forty of those same photocopied certificates by the time they reached ninth grade, and so would every other kid. It started to feel like all they had to do was show up to receive one. I eventually learned from the PTA about the *no one's a loser; everyone's a winner* concept. I was never really sure how this practice would prepare them for the real dog-eat-dog world out there, but that was their story, and they were sticking to it. I stopped worrying about flattening all those certificates or even preserving them, but I did store them in a big folder that remains up in the attic. Even though they weren't necessary for college applications, I figured they'd be fun to pull out someday when the kids are older. Artwork is also being saved in the big folder. How could we throw out their traced hands and the early pictures their teachers had them draw of us? I changed my hairdo based on some of those pictures that definitely reflected big hair.

Adding to the many emotional ups and downs we experienced during our kids' school years, was the struggle of whether to save them or let them sink. When we *again* found ourselves racing to the school to deliver the forgotten book or homework assignment we'd grumble, "This is the last time I'm doing this," and "They need to have a consequence for their disorganization and learn responsibility." Then the very next day your child came skipping in the door to report the field trip permission slip they brought home two weeks ago was due that day, and they were the only one in their homeroom who hadn't had it. Ouch! As you launched into your explanation you realized you had completely undone the lesson above.

How many times did we save them on their

projects due the next day instead of letting them sink? Did we really have a choice? The project, assigned six weeks before, still had four hours of work left and it was 9:00 p.m. So we entered the picture, like the white knight on the charging horse, assuring ourselves it was more important for them to get adequate sleep than to finish all the work themselves. We reminded them how many times we'd asked them to get going on this over the last six weeks, as we cut and paste away. There was no holding back the *I told you so*, even though we had, again, taken on the tone of our own parents' voices. We put our heart and soul into every last detail, making sure nothing was forgotten. T's were crossed, I's were dotted, and finally the project was finished. But here's the thing, after spending all that time cutting and pasting, we couldn't help but feel a certain ownership to the project. Right or wrong, it felt as much our project as our kid's. So we anxiously waited for the grading of our project, ah *their project*.

Right or wrong, it was devastating if we, ah,

they, got anything below a B. I never called to challenge these completely unreasonable grading decisions, but I sure did adjust my teachers' gifts accordingly. Oh, yes sirree.

Another strong emotion I'm positive we all experienced was the overwhelming feeling of seeing our children up on stage. They step up on that stage and all of a sudden the kids we lived with day in and day out, who needed direction to get through breakfast, looked like super stars. This was especially surprising considering the rampage at home beforehand to get them there.

Where are your black shoes?

Wasn't there a special shirt you had to wear?

One of your black shoes is where?

Then wear one of your brother's.

The shirt is in the bottom of your back pack?

You have to be there when?

I was supposed to bake?

Now you're flying into the auditorium because you also had to pick your other child up at the field after dropping this one off thirty minutes before the program, without baked goods. The parent with flowers and a helium balloon who slides into the row and sits right next to you surely brought baked goods. I remember rummaging through my purse for the Tootsie Roll I'd bought the day before from the Knights of Columbus to give to my son.... Hey, it was a king size! The show began and you had to duck around the stupid helium balloon floating into your line of vision.

You miss your child's one contribution to the evening because the camcorder isn't working. Okay, you haven't charged it since Easter. Your cell phone rings, startling you and everyone around you because your six-year-old changed the ring tone while she was waiting for the program to begin. This causes the people with the balloon to miss their child's one contribution to the evening, well, maybe that was okay...*and*...the program has your kid's name *misspelled*. But in the end you are bursting with pride seeing them up there on the stage, their face beaming with sheer joy at being part of something grand they will surely get a "form paper" certificate for. By the way, my son loved the Tootsie Roll.

Ladies and gentlemen, please, take it in and remember these incredible moments in our children's lives. Surely there is documented evidence somewhere in the attic. These were some of the very best moments of child rearing as well as some of the most challenging. This rite of passage for our children was as demanding for us, as parents, as it was for them. I know we wouldn't trade those years for the world, but I'd also bank on none of us really wanting to relive them. Thinking back, I can't imagine how we kept all those balls in the air. Some of it was youth, as we were younger and able to easily switch into autopilot, if necessary, and it *was* necessary. Some of it we simply made up along the way. Regardless, we did it, and here we are looking back at it all in awe of ourselves. Sure, the kids succeeded, but, remember, it's not about them right now. It's finally about us and our outstanding contribution to it all.

So this amazing milestone must be celebrated. Yes, by our children but also by us. After all the blood, sweat, and tears, day in and day out, for thirteen years you deserve a reward. Sooo, I have a little surprise for you. Long overdue is the opportunity to magnet a little something of your own on the refrigerator or even add it to a folder in the attic. Just do yourself a favor and don't wrinkle it, as the magazine article to flatten it is long gone.

SO IT IS MY GREAT HONOR TO PRESENT...

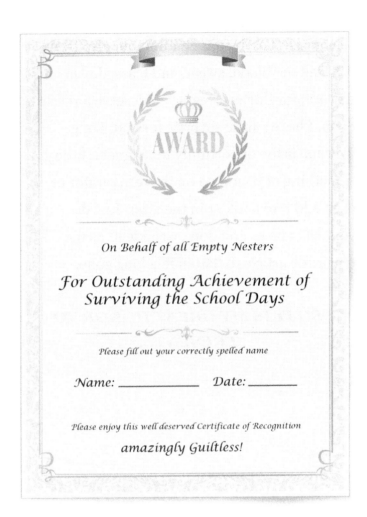

On Behalf of all Empty Nesters

For Outstanding Achievement of Surviving the School Days

Please fill out your correctly spelled name

Name: _____   Date: _____

Please enjoy this well deserved Certificate of Recognition

amazingly Guiltless!

Chapter Four
The Mutt

Dog lovers may consider skipping this chapter. Then again, a dog lover who happens to be realistic about the hassles of dog ownership, and I'm sure there are some, may read on. Even someone on the fence with this, should read on, as they are probably in denial and this could help. However, you will get the most out of *this* chapter if you are like me...badgered into dog ownership.

For those of us highly inconvenienced by dog ownership, it's hard to understand why some people feel a dog is essential to complete a human being's childhood. These dog lovers would never even consider raising their child without a hairy, tail-wagging mammal drooling and prancing through their living room every day. Nor do they complain about getting up from a comfortable position on the couch when the mutt is scratching at the door to go out every hour. Feeding, watering, walking, and especially scooping, is not a problem for them. I started to wonder if there was something wrong with me because I do feel so inconvenienced by it all. Then it hit me. I happen to be a goldfish lover. Basically, there are two kinds of people in this world: dog lovers and goldfish lovers, and that's just the way it is.

Goldfish are a snap. I feel guilty even counting them as a pet. Anyone who doesn't at least start with goldfish is showing off. Sprinkle a few food flakes in the water once a day, clean the bowl when you can't see through the glass...bing, bang, boom, you're done. This could go on for years, or at least the illusion of years.

With goldfish having such a short life span, they occasionally needed, well...replacing. When we found one floating belly up in the tank, we ran down to the nearest pet store and got another exactly like it before the kids were up from their naps or home from school. Flushed away the old, flopped in the new. No fuss, no muss. However, eventually the day arrived when the kids found the goldfish floating belly up and were surprisingly enthusiastic to send it swirling down the toilet bowl. How could they know about this? It usually meant your goldfish card had played out. There they stood with big sad puppy-dog eyes, not from losing the fish, but clutching the advertisement for the Humane Society dog kennel. Even if you attempted to head this off by dog sitting for the in-laws, it was hopeless. And if your spouse was on board with his own set of puppy-dog eyes, you were done.

So fellow goldfish lovers, when outnumbered and defeated on dog ownership, it was very important for us to at least have clear stipulations for getting one. My hard-and-fast rule was having the dog match the carpet. This was in anticipation of shedding which, by the way, people completely misled you on. They would say, "Oh, he's shedding now," making it seem like this was an occasional, probably seasonal event. Forget that. Dogs shed every minute of every day and in every season of the year. So my preempting this with matching carpet ended up being a genius move. I happened to get an almost-perfect match to my Medium Saddle Tan by Karastan with Daisy.

The PTA advised you should wait till your kids are a "good age" before adding a dog to your family. Did you happen to notice the wide range of opinions on what constituted a "good age?" Some said if you get a dog with babies then you have to be sure the dog doesn't hurt them, so wait till they're toddlers. Others said if you get a dog with toddlers, you have to make sure the toddler doesn't hurt the dog, better to get it when they're babies so they adjust. Then there was the delusional group suggesting if you get the dog when your kids are in elementary school they would be old enough to take responsibility for the care of the dog. Ha ha ha...but that's what we did.

So it was off to the Humane Society kennel to pick out a dog. If you used this venue to get your dog, then you know about the lengthy application and strict screening process involved. They made you feel like you should have dressed

the kids up for it and possibly done some
research on the best-rated dog foods available.
You first met the judgmental-looking person
behind the desk who proceeded to watch your
every move. Then you noticed how many other
families were walking around, kids dressed nice,
who you're evidently competing against. Your
stress level started to rise and you threatened the
kids about their behavior, fearing you wouldn't
pass. Even if you were like me and didn't really
want a dog, it became a matter of principle to
measure up. I also remember one moment of
panic during our interview when we did not have
a reference from a veterinarian. We didn't need
one for the goldfish. The interviewer's look of
disdain told us we were on very shaky ground.
The kids were in the background making fun of
the three-legged cat hobbling around, putting
our chance of dog ownership even more at risk.
But, somehow, for reasons unbeknown to me, we
were deemed acceptable. Driving home, I
couldn't help think how we never went through
any kind of interrogation to bear children.

Of course we didn't bring the dog home that day.

No, the dog, who was there due to abandonment stayed until you returned with proof of appropriate preparedness to bring it home. They have you sign an agreement committing to follow through with this before leaving the premises. This is the only way they will save the right-colored dog for you.

They sent us home with a complete list of all the items we would need. I'd had no idea getting a dog would be so involved. We brought the fish home in a baggie.

So, off to the pet shop we went. The dog section is very different from the fish section, with aisle after aisle of unbelievable products. They featured apparel, grooming products, entertainment items, and a selection of feeding accessories to name a few. Tutorials on housebreaking and incontinence were being offered every two hours. I even saw a display of bark-control items. We can do that? It became very clear, very quickly we were entering a whole new dog-ownership world. Actually, it felt more like a secret club, where all the members gave each other knowing looks of recognition and understanding. "Look at this," one of them would say pointing to a dog treat shaped like a squirrel on a stick, sprinkled with colored jimmies, as the other squealed in delight. Others were discussing what kind of Sniffany & Co. dog toy they should purchase.

Some browsed around quietly with blissful smiles, taking in the sheer magic of the dog-centric environment.

I controlled my urge to confront them with reality. They were discussing a mutt, and it would never be responsible for putting them in a nice nursing home someday. Think back now, back to when we were kids....

Our dogs came from one of our parents' friends who was trying to get rid of a litter, or a stray showed up at our back door. Our parents did not fill out an application and go for an interview. Can you imagine them doing that? Didn't we find a stick in the yard and throw it around for the dog to fetch? A stick right? Not a $14.99 Nylabone knot to prevent plaque buildup and strengthen gums.

Didn't we feed our childhood dogs table scraps once a day in the oldest plastic bowl from the back of the kitchen cupboard? *Not* a complete and nutritionally balanced dog food with probiotics for superior digestibility, with skin and coat conditioners for $25.00 a bag. That we served in a $19.99 nonskid, ergonomically correct dog dish. I often wondered how the Hamburger Helper, on Corelle, I served the kids for dinner measured up.

Didn't we just throw an old blanket down on the floor for our dogs when they did come in the house? *Not* a specialized flea-resistant, fleece bed with memory foam, for $89.99. After they grew out of the $150.00 crate in six months.

At least I put my foot down on the doggie cardigan with matching hat. I also made a mental note to encourage the kids to consider opening a pet shop as a lucrative career option one day. Secure in its pewter epoxy powder-coated crate, with dual-slide bolt latches, the puppy is finally given clearance to come with you. Puppies are very overwhelmed with the change of environment and constant attention of doting children when they first come into a home. This resulted in their peeing uncontrollably every fifteen to twenty minutes, forcing us to begin housebreaking them right off the bat. The information the Humane Society provided outlined many different techniques. It reminded me a lot of potty training the kids. My husband, a dog lover, took the lead on this. He preferred the technique of bringing the puppy's nose to the puddle, smacking a newspaper violently on the floor beside the puddle, followed by yelling at the top of his lungs, while our three kids looked on in terror. I can't imagine what technique he would have used if he was a goldfish lover. I do know therapy would have been needed for the kids. Like potty training, regardless of what technique you use, the puppy became housebroken when the puppy decided it wanted to.

You also had to make a veterinarian appointment as soon as you get your dog home. This was clearly stated in the Humane Society agreement you signed. If you're still with me, dog lovers, you're really not going to like this part. I found the veterinarian visits to be even more exasperating than the pet store. The people working there not only seemed to be extremely into animals, they actually resembled them. It was amazing and unsettling. For instance, wasn't there usually a long and bushy-haired veterinary assistant lumbering around, shaking her hair out from time to time, a little round shouldered, kind of resembling a German Shepherd? And wasn't there always a mousy receptionist with a squeaky little voice? Even the veterinarians themselves would slowly slink into the room in a cat-like way. They let every dog lick their faces to smithereens and called them doggie kisses. And maybe it was my mind playing tricks, but I could have sworn they were all snacking from the bowl of dog treats sitting on the counter.

Also, whose idea was it to mix all the animals

up in the waiting room? I thought those people were experts. Did they really expect dogs and cats to amiably sit next to each other and forget they were enemies? And if a bird showed up, forget it. Now it was like Wild Kingdom in a twelve-by-twelve room. Then there were the animal owners who thought we were thrilled their animal was sniffing, licking, jumping on, or humping our leg while we waited for our appointment. They wore big old grins of pride as their animals basically molested us. Meanwhile, I wanted to scream "Why would you think I like your animal when I barely like my own! Besides, I don't even let my husband do what your mutt is doing there."

Once safely in the exam room, I couldn't help but question the number of vaccinations they recommended. Why would a dog need four different shots averaging $60.00 each? It wasn't like she was traveling abroad or living in a sewer. They seemed concerned by my response, as well as my follow-up question, "Don't we just let nature take its course with animals?" They soon figured out I was only there to find out what they had to prevent the dog from getting fleas. I did notice the mousy receptionist add my name to some list on the way out. Whatever....

Adding to the trauma of vet visits is the car ride to get them there. Some dogs can't handle this. If your dog was one of them, then you know all about the jumping, panting over your shoulder, and drooling down your back while driving. Funny how they warn you about the dangers of driving while eating, they fine you for driving while using a cell phone, but driving with a crazy dog in the car is evidently fine. Like that wasn't distracting! There wasn't a dog toy in that pet store able to calm a dog hyper about car rides, not even one by Sniffany & Co.

Then came the day when you had no choice but to book a boarding kennel for your dog after exhausting or abusing all other dog-sitting options. Finding a kennel was easy but dropping off the dog there was not. I found myself having a conversation with our dog while she was trampolining in the backseat, trying to prepare her for the experience. As I walked in with her blanket, toys, favorite food, and sound track of the family at dinner, I worried about how this will all be so very different for her.

There would be unfamiliar faces, a new environment, and she would be in the company of other dogs all day. She had been an only dog her whole life. I didn't see a smidge of carpet anywhere, and she'd gotten so used to the wall to wall Medium Saddle Tan in our home. How about the spot behind her ear we scratch to calm her down, would they do that? Would they give her any attention at all? Luckily, our dog would happily greet the staff and willingly follow them to that place in the back of the building where she'd stay, day in and day out, for the next seven days. I don't know about you, but I never quite had the nerve to actually look at "that place." I went with blind trust, convincing myself all the barking I heard was happy dogs, doing happy things.

Whoever expected to experience separation anxiety when dropping a dog off at a kennel?

This took me completely by surprise. I never felt this when I left the goldfish. So there you were after not wanting a dog in the first place, but still going through the rituals of housebreaking, poop scooping, hair vacuuming, and, reluctantly, shots. Low and behold, you're attached. Funny how the kids, who desperately wanted the dog, said a quick bye and skipped out of the kennel without a worry in the world. They didn't worry because they knew you were worried sick. That's what we do as parents, we worry about everything, so our kids don't have a care in the world.

Thing is, while the kids are out living their carefree "non-poop-scooping lives," many of us go on caring for their dog for years. They come home to visit, ooh and aah over them then off they go again, back to their "dog-dander-free" lives. Basically, we were conned. We were conned by the pet store, by the veterinarian, and by our very own kids. We can't even call ourselves Empty Nesters if we're stuck with the mutt that, by no fault of our own, we're attached to. We have only one option...revenge! Come on, deep breath, you can do this.

First. No more kennels. Plan a little getaway and get the kids to stay with the dog. Don't take no for an answer. Tapping into good ol' parental guilt works well here. "But the poor thing is showing signs of depression, moping around and barely eating." "We don't dare chance the kennel as we never found out what really goes on in 'that place.'" "The vet suggested spending time with the kids would perk her up."

Done!

Second. Hit 'em where it hurts: "Hi honey, oh the dog is fine but we just got a $350.00 bill from the vet for her. She now needs a very expensive senior vitamin-fortified dog food and a prescription for Prozac." Seal the deal with, "So do you mind using *your* money for those sneakers you wanted?" Ouch.

Third, but most important. Weekly dog stories. Updates emphasizing all you're doing for it. Example: "The dog got into the trash three times this week and we had to buy two new covered trash cans." Don't hold back on the details. "The trash was strewn from one end of the kitchen to the other, with coffee grounds everywhere." Have fun with it. "It looked like a nuclear waste site in need of a hazmat clean up." Now bring it home. "We're still having nightmares."

Perfect!

Now wasn't that fun? Would you have ever considered revenge as a reward? Well, in this book, it is. You're simply cashing in on all those years of caring for the dog. Even though, as hard as it is to admit, our dogs have added an element of companionship to our lives the goldfish probably wouldn't have. We must still never forget mutts are, and always have been, optional.

So, for all of us who went over and above the parental call of duty and took on the trials and tribulations of dog ownership, it's time to savor the reward of sweet revenge!

And do it...

amazingly Guiltless!

Chapter Five
Wild World of Sports

Sports used to be optional for children, not anymore.

Our generation assumed every kid would play a sport. Some got away with the arts, but they had to have a very good excuse. "I'm a descendent of Picasso," or "My uncle is Billy Joel" would possibly suffice. Otherwise, the expectation was all kids would be part of the wild world of sports.

Signups for sports occurred two seasons before the sport began, which explained why most kids lost interest in it by the first practice. Getting brand new cleats would sometimes spur their enthusiasm. If they fit into a pair in the garage, it only added to the kid's diminished zeal.

Forgetting to check for spiders in those garage cleats would sabotage the operation. I used to kick myself when I forgot to do a spider sweep. Sometimes the search for cleats became a neighborhood project with parents exploring each other's garages to see what sizes they had. That was why firstborn children were not exempt from using old cleats. It was also not unheard of to contact out-of-state cousins to see what sizes they had lying around. I'm not really sure of the psychology behind our extreme efforts to avoid buying new cleats for our kids each sports season, but it might have something to do with mud. The new cleats looked just like the old cleats after the first practice. Mud was always an issue with the early-season practices held in fields where a foot of snow had recently melted, or two inches of rain had poured on. Things really didn't dry up until mid-season, and nobody was going to waste their money on buying new cleats then. By that point it was a struggle to get a kid to go at all. If not for the promise of a hot dog at the end of the game, no one would show up after mid-season.

Making our kids show up dutifully for their sport was our way of teaching them the lessons of team responsibilities. "The team is counting on you," we would say. "Being on a team is a commitment."

Unfortunately, by teaching them these lessons of responsibility and commitment, we also compromised the lessons of priorities and using good judgment. Because the team was counting on them they missed homework assignments, dental appointments, and family celebrations. Because they had a commitment to the team, they went to bed too late, ate too much junk food at the concession stand, and ran around in the rain for hours without the proper clothes. To fulfill their responsibilities to the team, they went to practices sick and with sprained ankles wrapped in ace bandages. I guess we went along with this because, as parents, we were also reeled in on the team responsibility effect. It started in the bleachers of the first game when the lady with the clipboard made her way around. Remember the clipboard lady? She had more charts on that clipboard than NFL coaches have on the sideline. Turned out our names had to be entered in numerous blank spaces on her charts, committing our time to a variety of parent jobs. She explained this with a glare we hadn't seen since being called to the principal's office in third grade, "The league can't go on unless parents do their part." All along we thought our part was signing up, paying the fees, buying the equipment and uniforms, sometimes cleats, getting them to and from the practices, and cheering at the games. Wrong, there were also parent jobs. So as the clipboard lady stood before us, and we felt the stares of all the other parents in the bleachers, our minds were desperately trying to visualize the kitchen calendar at home. We never made any commitments without checking the kitchen calendar. That thing was the Mission Control of life, Grand Central Station, the hub of our existence. Suddenly we're scribbling our name into all the Tuesday spots. We hoped this made us appear organized and on top of things.

Meanwhile, we had absolutely no idea what was going on Tuesdays without seeing our calendar. But since the clipboard lady was usually the coach's wife, we certainly didn't want to hesitate. We heard from the PTA how important it was to cooperate with coaches, as any slip up could affect a kid's playing time. Before moving on to the next victim, I mean parent, she handed us a five-pound manila envelope. Probably instructions for our parent jobs right? Nope. As we collected ourselves enough to focus on the bold, ominous writing at the top of the envelope, there it was...*Fundraiser*.

Once home in the safety of our kitchen, we began to comb through the twenty-five pages of fundraiser material in the envelope. Turned out twenty of the twenty-five pages are about the prizes our child will win if they sell a minimum of thirty boxes of candy and nuts. The thirty-sold item range had things like high-frequency sonic yoyos and huge super-soaker Nerf guns. The fifty-item range had radio-controlled cars and electric keyboards. The kind of stuff we would typically give our child for Christmas or their birthday. We certainly couldn't let the kids see this. After all, we just sent back the manila envelope for the second fundraiser of the year to the school.

That one tapped out all our relatives and friends as well as people we pretended were our friends. We were wishing we had cultivated relationships with the neighbors farther down the street and kept in better touch with our cousins in Youngstown. As we're contemplating all this and continuing to skim through the remaining material, suddenly the words *Buy Out* jump out at us. It seemed for the Buy Out option, we simply paid a ridiculous dollar amount and were then immediately off the hook. We considered this, even though our child's prize would be a pencil with a smiley face on it. We wonder if this counts as "doing our part," but figure for as much as they're ripping us off, it must. Besides it was still better than buying the thirty-item minimum and giving everyone turtle caramels for Christmas. It hurt to write the check, but we found it helped to keep chanting, "I have to do my part. I have to do my part." We thought we were all set until our son came home from practice ranting about James getting a karaoke machine for his fundraising, and all he got was a stupid pencil. This is when we teach our child the lesson of "life isn't always fair." We also found out that most of those Tuesday spots we filled in were to work the concession stand. Life really wasn't fair! Why couldn't we have gotten cutting up oranges at halftime or washing the team pinnies. Nope, you were assigned the grueling job of concession stand. Now if you were lucky enough to get the cashier/candy counter in the concession stand, we were somewhat spared. But if you got the grilling job cooking fried dough and flipped burgers all day, it meant coming home covered head to toe in grease. It would take two shampoos to get it out of your hair, even your contacts were coated. On the positive side, that griddle grease was most likely a very effective anti-aging skin treatment, way before we were even looking for one.

Remember how intense the concession stand got with the after-game rush, or when you ran out of ring pops. Ring pops were essential to getting younger siblings through the game. I used to feel terrible when I had to look a desperate parent in the eye and say, "We're out of ring pops."

The only good thing about working the concession stand was it gave us a break from sitting in the bleachers with the other parents. Yeah, I know, they were the parents of our kids' friends, and it was good to get to know them. But by the end of the season we knew way more about their lives than we ever wanted to. Some of these parents used game time bleacher conversation as their own personal therapy session. We heard great details about their Aunt Rosalie in Denver, who was causing havoc in the family by not wanting to make the trip for the annual reunion. "Can you believe it? She only has to get on a plane and we'd be right there to pick her up." "We even have a bedroom set up for her on the first floor." "It's probably because she had that disagreement with Uncle Ron." This was all discussed in a tone of complete exasperation, in a volume heard by everyone in the bleachers. Soon everyone on the bleachers weighed in with their opinions. It became a very involved conversation with many different views discussed. Before we knew it, everyone had missed their kid make their hit, goal, basket, point, or whatever they were supposed to make. Missing our kids perform due to bleacher conversation was a touchy situation and had to be handled very carefully. The technique most often agreed upon by the parents was to deny it and tell them you saw every second.

Of course, there were always the few parents that would completely ignore the running conversations in the bleachers. They were the die-hard sports parents who instead of helping with the discussion about someone's life dilemma, bellowed at the top of their lungs through the whole game. I could never tell whether their kid was doing good because the desperate tone in their voice never changed. Even when their child completely missed the ball in a Little League game, they would yell out an ear piercing "Good cut! Good swing." My seventy-year-old father sat at one of those games, leaned over to me and asked, "Don't they ever say, 'You Missed the damn ball'?" Once again, our parents didn't need this book. Anyway, those die-hard parents behaved as if their helpful advice from the sidelines would result in their kid's picture on a Wheaties box someday. They were also the parents who showed up at the end of season banquet in suit and tie, as if it would help secure their kid's spot on a good team the next year.

We all had our moments of exuberance when our kids did something wonderful in their sporting events. And if we weren't distracted by the bleacher conversation, we'd bellow out a "Good job" cheer. Those are the moments that gave us the momentum to get through the season. We just knew better than to let it go to our heads. Not so for the die-hard sports parents. I heard they even got their kids *new* cleats every year. Crazy, I tell you.

But let's not forget the moments when we

felt our children were wronged. This tapped into the very core of our parental instincts. It took the utmost self-control to handle these situations correctly. Most of us started out, offering a nice comment like, "Oh wow, my kid is still sitting out," in a calm voice but loud enough for the clipboard lady to hear. We hoped our comment would be relayed back to her husband, the coach, during dinner that night. If the passive approach didn't work, passive-aggressive was only a stone's throw away. A ding in the coach's new Lexus side panel could happen by accident. "Wow, must have been gravel, Coach. So how's it going with all the kids' playing time?" We did, however, want to avoid at all costs resorting to a completely aggressive approach. Irate screaming and throwing things at the coach with a security escort to the parking lot never ended well. Kids would threaten to drop out of school from embarrassment and spouses wouldn't talk to us for months. Then again, if we had to, we had to.

We all remember the sports banquets, though. How could we not? A celebration the season had ended and we finally got our lives back. However, this was the last episode of the bleacher-conversation dilemmas, so we wanted to carefully pick a seat at the right table to be able to hear the final episode. Getting stuck at the table with the die-hard, over-dressed sports parent, would make for a very long evening. They would spend the evening recapping the highlights of their kid's season. It always amazed me how these banquets were held in banquet facilities designed for wedding receptions, when we were accommodating a clientele who preferred pizza and chicken nuggets as a menu choice. They had cloth tablecloths, a full service of silverware, and waiters who swept into the room with the salad course. An adult was asked to sit at each table so the kids didn't throw dinner rolls at each other. But there we sat, with balloon centerpieces, the filmed season running on a large screen in the corner, and a display of each player's baby picture. I was never really sure what baby pictures had to do with sports. The master of ceremonies would get things going with a speech. Then the head of the league rose to honor us with a speech. The head coach talked about the season with a speech. And then the assistant coach gave his version of the season with a speech. Not to knock their aptitude for public speaking, but just one decent joke would have helped.

Then each player received a trophy and life-size action-shot poster of themselves. This is when we realized where the fundraising money went. And then, right when it appeared things were winding down, they threw in special awards: Most Valuable Player, Rookie of the Year, Team Spirit, Captain's Award, Merit Award...each with a little speech.

Team gifts followed with each kid receiving a team hoodie or duffle bag with their name embroidered on it. This is when we realized why the banquet was $35.00 a head. Finally, as the waiters dozed in the corner...it was over.

How did we get to this point? Somewhere between watching *Reading Rainbow* and playing with Legos for hours on the family-room floor, someone came up with "You have to keep kids busy." Don't you wish it could be more like when we were their age? If we wanted to play you showed up at the open field down the street, or the kid's house with the biggest backyard. We divided into teams without tryouts or $40.00 uniforms and got through the game without a coach or even a whistle. Sure, sometimes there were fights, and occasionally the game fell apart, but we figured it out because we wanted to play. Gone are the days of pick-up games where kids got their first punch in the nose, a childhood rite of passage, because someone was mad about losing. There were no adults interfering, in fact the adults didn't even know about it. Honestly, our parents didn't want to know about it, as long as we were home in time for dinner.

We were the generation of parents who organized every minute of play for our kids and brought it to a whole new level of importance. As if that wasn't enough, someone came up with team bondings, which consisted of pasta dinners for the players the night before a game. The carbs were guaranteed to help the players perform better, along with being bonded. Parents were expected to provide the dinners in their home, on a weeknight. All thirty teammates attended. I don't know of anyone who ever offered to do a second team bonding. So, as we attempted to squeeze all this in around the essential routines of our everyday lives, we ended up with parents and kids on overload. Also, the next generation of parents are even surpassing us.

They wouldn't think of not selling enough fundraiser items for their kids to come home with an electronic prize...no smiley pencils happening there. And as far as their banquets, they've added make-your-own-sundae buffets, photo booths, and they all show up wearing suits.

But we Empty Nesters know exactly how the story ends. The trophies will end up in a box in the closet and the team picture in the bottom of a drawer. The kids won't want to carry the monogrammed duffle bag or wear the team hoodie after the season ends. But mostly we know those die-hard sports parents really need to *lose the suit*, because it really doesn't matter. The kids will look back at all this as a little something they did for a while when they were children. If asked now, they probably wouldn't even remember there were balloons at the banquets. The only real lasting impression they will have is getting a smiley-face pencil instead of a radio-controlled car.

We could make ourselves crazy thinking about the over-the-moon kids' sports attitude we all bought into, or we could put our energy toward rewarding ourselves for actually getting through it. You know where I'm going with this. In fact, after remembering all that went into sports for the kids, I bet you already have ideas. By the way, you happen to be making very good progress with the *guiltless* part of this book. Are you thinking the arts? Of course, getting tickets to a non-sports event is just the medicine we need. Entertainment on a stage instead of a field, court, pool, or track! Somewhere offering cocktails instead of ring pops. Seats with cushioned backs in a venue with a climate-controlled atmosphere. The world outside our kids' sporting activities we didn't make time for while twirling around their schedules. I'm talking dressing up and maybe a little dinner beforehand. The arts are out there waiting for us to indulge. It's finally our turn to take the ball and run with it. Ticketmaster, here we come!

And do it...

amazingly Guiltless!

Chapter Six
Vacation Bonding

Make no mistake, a vacation with the kids was great if you had the strength to prepare for it and endurance to execute it. It was not for the weak or feebleminded. Part of our generation's kid-pleaser parenting method included providing regular vacation experiences for our children. I don't know about you, but *vacation experiences* during my childhood were few and far between, usually involving a visit to the relatives in Ohio for a few nights. One year we actually went to Lake Erie for a week with my cousins. But after my mom forgot a laundry basket, yes laundry basket, of our clothes and we had to buy some, my dad wouldn't let us go anywhere ever again. Parenting magazines outlined a multitude of suggestions for family vacations for our generation of parents, and made it very clear we better come through on this. The pressure from all the propaganda was impossible to ignore. The PTA even encouraged vacations for providing valuable family-bonding time. I guess living in the same house, sharing everything from couches, televisions, and toasters to towels, bathrooms, and sometimes bedrooms didn't count.

There were two approaches for planning family vacations. The first was the democratic approach of getting input from all family members and collaborating on a decision. Yes, everyone researching, discussing, and then coming to an agreement. The parenting magazines wholeheartedly backed this one as a beneficial part of the bonding experience. Fortunately, we tested the democratic approach on a day trip to the beach before using it on a real vacation. The democratic discussion at the kitchen table resulted in one kid sobbing, another refusing to go, and the third throwing the map across the room, taking out a row of violets on the window sill. Clearly, the theory had *not* been well researched or fully tested. We should have known better, as this didn't even work in the grocery store when trying to get the kids to pick out a box of cereal. What those parenting magazines didn't consider was no two people in any family have the same idea about what they want for a vacation or for breakfast. The democratic approach was a recipe for disaster that even the perfect Walton family couldn't have resolved without John-Boy getting his knickers in a twist.

The second, and more practicable method, was the dictatorial approach where the parents do the research, the parents have the discussions, and the parents decide where the family is vacationing.

The children are then told where they are going and sometimes not until they are carried from their beds, in the wee hours of the morning, and belted into the car. Yup, just "Here's where you're going." We chose this approach figuring we'd bond later.

The moment the vacation is booked, the packing process begins. I am quite certain the concept of "the list" originated as a result of vacation packing. At no other time in life was it as important to organize your thoughts into a linear structure. To attempt to pack without a list is seriously mad, and composing it became the whole focus of your existence. If you thought of something to pack while vacuuming, you stopped and wrote it on the list. If a thought came to you in the middle of the night, out of bed you'd jump to add it to the list. Even when out doing errands or at work, if something came to mind you'd scribble it on a checkbook deposit slip until it could be entered on the list. The confidence the list gave you was invaluable as you took on the overwhelming task of packing up life for an entire family. Some would say, "Well, they do have stores there if you forget something." How dare they downplay the value of the list. That's like saying if you forget your new bathing suit, after spending four hours trying on thirty-seven of them, you can just jump into a store and grab one.

Ridiculous! How about your favorite orange sun visor and fanny pack, two must-haves on any vacation. Do they think you can find them in any store? Outrageous. I ignored them.

Life stood still in our house when the actual vacation packing began. Dinners were batch-up meals, mostly using up food in the refrigerator. Also, no wearing packable clothes and underwear for two weeks before the vacation, only the old, faded stuff. This was when we realized how much of the family's wardrobe actually fell into the category. Even though everyone's been wearing those same clothes without a thought, laying them out to put in a suitcase throws a whole new light on them. Because of this mandatory clothes ceiling, social engagements during the packing process were also out. "Sorry, I'd love to join you but I'm going on vacation in two weeks and I'm packing." Not everyone understood this, and sometimes the explanation was received with duress. Usually by people who were packing challenged, the no "list" people...I ignored them.

Our families never really appreciated the time and effort that went into packing them up for a vacation. In fact, my family began calling me the packing bully. Yup, no appreciation at all. But, guaranteed, at some point in the vacation when they needed a safety pin or nail clipper, I was right there with it. Yes, indeed, the old packing bully came through. I ignored them, too.

Not only was it necessary to plan for the things needed on the vacation, but there was getting to the vacation to think about as well. The kids' entertainment bag for traveling was crucial. Even if we were only on the road for a few hours, this bag had to be fully equipped. Funny how when we were kids the only entertainment we had in a car was dangling stuff out the back of the station wagon, if we were lucky enough to get the back. Otherwise, we searched for out-of-state license plates on passing cars or counted cows. But, the generation of kids we were rearing had been kept busier than ever with their sports and school activities, so they are completely unaccustomed to sitting still and staring out a car window. Even something as cool as hanging a string out the back of a station wagon would not cut it for today's kid. This put pressure on parents to be very comprehensive in packing their traveling entertainment bags. You had to consider each child's individual personality. The readers were easiest. A couple of their favorite books would usually do it with a backup *I Spy* book. The artistic kids were more complicated. They needed one of every one hundred thirty-three Crayola crayon colors along with an array of colored pencils to accent them, two packs of three-hundred-count paper, and a lap tabletop. The girl's bags definitely had the most small parts.

Barbie doll accessories, tiny Polly Pocket pieces, little brushes for their My Little Pony, and tiny beads for string bracelets. But whatever it took to get through the car ride to get to a vacation destination was well worth the trouble. I remember what a traveling breakthrough it was when the Walkman came out and all we had to do was plug in each kid. Today's parents have it even better with DVD players built into their cars. Two Disney flicks and they're there. No challenge at all! Eventually, the carefully thought out entertainment bag was no longer entertaining. The clue was the accidental elbow-to-elbow encounter in the backseat resulting in a scream like someone losing a limb. This signaled one parent to sit in the backseat to referee and begin directing the entertainment. I once cranked a wind-up radio singing "It's a Small World" three hundred ninety-five times on a trip to Pittsburgh. It took three hours, after our arrival, to get the song out of my head. Remember the day you made it through an entire trip without having to leave the front seat? Oh, glorious day! It may have coincided with the Walkmans. But, until then, pit stops helped.

Our pit stops rivaled those of NASCAR with gassing up, a potty break, quick repacking of entertainment bags, and a speedy return to the road. I could dig Barbie shoes and crayons out of seats in record time. I reorganized the entire backseat that looked as though the entertainment bag detonated and had those kids back in their belts by the time the gas tank was full. It was extremely important not to let pit stops become snack time, and waste a valuable time killer while on the road. Even though en route snacks took a considerable amount of set up and dispensing, it was worth it. Twizzlers were the best, as they required a lot of chewing, keeping their mouths busy, and no crumbs. But even the crumbs were worth it for a good half hour of quiet. Juice boxes were marketed as great for a car trip, but we all know what that resulted in. Juice squirting all over a sibling and lost straws. Another idea not properly researched or fully tested.

Vacation snacks were usually things we normally didn't allow our kids to have in real life. This probably explains why our kids were ravenous 90 percent of the time while on vacation. You'd think the novelty of being somewhere different would distract them from their hunger...just not so. Again, pressure from the propaganda played into this as there are reminders to eat everywhere you go. Science museums offered candy items in the shape of robots. Historical attractions had pretzels in the shape of Abe Lincoln's head. And amusement parks were the worst, with blinking neon signs advertising food items at every turn. Foods that once in a stomach couldn't possibly make it through the swirling, dipping, upside-downing rides. This explains why food, along with the gift shop, often became the main focus for our kids on vacation. At least we could use gift shops to our advantage.

The bribe of a visit to the gift shop could even get a kid through the turbo-engine display at the Smithsonian.

Unfortunately, we all learned the hard way what happens when we allowed our kids to run freely through the gift shop. Yup, you found them staring up at the $80.00, five-foot-long stuffed seal, thinking they couldn't live without it. If you kept on top of them you could instead navigate them over to the $2.99 rope bracelets. I could sell those rope bracelets like nobody's business. It got to the point that other customers started to wander over and consider them. I had everyone convinced it was the perfect keepsake to remember an amusement park or the Smithsonian.

Beach vacations with kids were always the most difficult for me. For some reason they were the number-one suggested family vacation from the propaganda ads. What those ads didn't tell us was the amount of stuff needed for the family beach experience. It required a "list" all its own. It also took everyone in the car carrying as much as they could, along with strangers who picked up the things we dropped, just to get everything from your car to the beach.

Even the two-year-old had a few things draped over her. The propaganda ads also left out the sand issues. You know, how the sand ends up in everything, and I mean *everything*! Drinks, food, teeth, as well as embedded deep into the fibers of towels. They also don't mention how it buries car keys and the six-year-old's favorite Tweety sunglasses. By the end of the day it has even worked its way into certain orifices of the human body. They don't mention how beach umbrellas never stay up and rafts never stay inflated. How seagulls dive bomb your head while you're eating lunch and the ocean breeze blows all the sandwich wrappers into the water, which triggers a lecture from outraged kids on protecting the environment. The bathrooms were a mile and a half away and the kids refused to pee in the ocean, again the environment. The highlight, however, was always when I lost sight of one of the kids and ran frantically up and down the beach, heart pounding out of my chest, until I found them making a sand castle with another family...that's right, *bonding!*

And why on earth did we take our babies to the beach? Really now, why? We could have sat them up in front of a mural of an ocean in the family room and gotten the same results, without sandy diapers.

But no, we all had to get the picture of daddy dipping baby's feet in the freezing-cold ocean water, while baby screams bloody murder. Did any of us ever consider what it did to their poor little bodies? They spent nine months in a 98.6

degree womb and then mostly a climate-controlled environment until the time of their dousing. This would be considered child abuse in some cultures. When we were babies, we certainly were not tortured like this. Our parents didn't feel the need to photograph their baby's feet in the ocean. Again, our parents did not need this book.

The propaganda advertisements made it look un-American if we didn't want to have beach experiences with our kids. It was equivalent to not voting or flag burning.

People would passionately ask, as I flushed the sand out of my eyes in the beach shower, "Don't you just love the beach?!" In other words, you're a real numbskull if you don't. Just to be clear, it isn't that I don't appreciate the beauty of the ocean and a beach, it's more about being submersed in them. I love looking at clouds, but I don't necessarily want to float in them. Due to my patriotism, and pressure from the propaganda, our kids got their fair share of beach experiences. Although I mostly remember my jubilance at getting back in the car and feeling the vinyl seats and floor mats. God Bless America!

For many families, the ultimate vacation with the kids is the "Disney experience." These trips were frequently planned around school vacations, as we tried to be responsible parents by prioritizing studies before play. This would have been a great idea if three quarters of the country didn't have the same idea. So, as responsible parents we paid higher air fares, higher admissions, and a higher price for our accommodations. The three miles of winding, waiting stalls at each attraction were put there just for school vacation weeks. Disney tries to make you think you aren't waiting an hour and a half by entertaining you during the wait, but that only works for the first thirty minutes. Looking back, would it have changed anything at all in our kids' lives today if we had taken them out of school for a lousy five days, saved $1,500.00, and seen twice as many attractions? I'm thinking not.

Vacations like Disney involved the added stress of keeping track of everyone's individual entrance card. Your entire $4,000.00 vacation was wrapped up in a 2" x 3" plastic card. Handing this valuable card over to a five-year-old to swipe was terrifying, but talking them out of doing it themselves was impossible. Impossible, without holding up the line for an extra thirty minutes and make a complete spectacle of the family. So, to avoid mayhem, I just held my breath through the swipe then immediately grabbed it out of her hand. Sounds foolproof, but you know how quickly things can go wrong in the life of a five-year-old. How it ended up teetering on the railing of Splash Mountain that day, I will never know.

Some families went the outdoorsy route for their family vacation. Camping was also propagandized as another great bonding option and very affordable. That is, before adding in the mini golf, bumper cars, and arcade visits necessary to get kids through a week of camping. No kid is happy just sitting in the woods for very long. Once the novelty of telling stories by the fire, sleeping in a tent, and catching lightning bugs wears off, they were begging for the old familiar sensory-overload type entertainment. We also had to figure in a trip to a Laundromat and a night at the Holiday Inn if it poured rain. Probably the purchase of some firewood for the end of the week, as well, when the entire family flat refused to hunt for it anymore. Being situated near a lake helped in keeping the kids happy, barring a child afraid of touching anything associated with fish or floating objects resembling fish. Why did everything have a catch?

Then there was the vacation picture taker...every family had one. It's easy to know who it was because there are no pictures of them anywhere. Usually the vacation picture taker took his role very seriously. He would go to great lengths to get the shot right. "Look. Smile. Hold on. Okay, smile. Wait a minute. Move over a little. Now smile. Just one more. Look this way. Stop it with the fingers over his head. Now look.

Ready. Say pizza. Good, good. Ok, one more. Really. Over here by the tree. Will you stop goofing around? Ready? Don't move. Say cheese. What a memory this will be." By the time the photo sessions were over, everyone was completely disgusted with the vacation picture taker, in a bad mood, and hungry again.

So to the generation of parents who planned and packed, and listened to the advice of the propaganda to bond our families with family vacations, listen up. It's time to buy a magazine titled *Couple's Escape*. The one you haven't dared to glance at for years. Well, it's now time to take a glance. In fact, it's time to do this. These places are like paradise. Notice the expressions of pure delight on the couples in the ads. Now that's the kind of propaganda I can go for. If you choose something with a beach think how easy it will be. No sandy footprints on your towel or kids begging you to bury their feet. If you choose to drive, no entertainment bags to pack. A vacation without tantrums in the gift shop and exhibits you can read without your leg being tugged.

Think how packing for just the two of you will be.

Now, don't get carried away. You will still need "the list." Also, expect to feel a little unsettled at first. It's inevitable after all the years of family vacationing. In fact, there are stages of adjustment for this:

Stage One: Gloominess & worry…missing and worrying about the kids.

Stage Two: *Guilt*…there's no getting out of it.

Stage Three: Realization…. Hey, wait a minute, I'm enjoying myself.

Stage Four: Embracing…really digging your teeth into the vacation now.

Stage Five: *Guilt* again…because you haven't thought about the kids all day.

Stage Six: Souvenir shopping…alleviates stage five.

Stage Seven: Elation…. You are absolutely loving this!

Think you can do this? The answer should be an enthusiastic *yes*. Come on, simply Google Couples Escape and type in your credit card. The 2" x 3" plastic admission card will be in the safety of *your* hands in no time. What a memory this will be! After all those years of listening to the propaganda and bonding with your family on vacation, it's now time to reward yourself with a vacation just for *you*!

And do it...

***amazingly* Guiltless !**

Chapter Seven
Holiday Hoopla

The kickoff to the holiday season every year was, of course, the picture for the holiday card. Preparations for this picture started the minute the Halloween costumes hit the floor after trick or treating. Procrastination would risk a holiday picture card arriving in the embarrassing window between Christmas and New Year's.

Those cards were sent by the people who could not get their act together. None of us wanted to be in that group. To get this project off the ground, we needed to schedule it, we needed to outfit it, and we needed to establish bribes to assure execution of the plan. With this came a whole array of challenges to work around.

Take scheduling, for instance. If you scheduled the picture during nap time, mealtime, or Barney time, you were skunked. The holiday-card picture absolutely, positively had to be scheduled when your child had no emotional, recreational, or bodily needs. Since all children in our time zone were on a similar schedule, you had to be aggressive in getting the sought-after hours in the morning or afternoon optimal for picture taking. I know they offered a discount for the times of day Barney was on, but I never chanced it.

Another challenge was coordinating outfits for the holiday picture. Finding the right size, in the correct holiday colors, often involved visiting several different locations of the same store. If we changed stores, the color palettes would not match up, as no two stores carry the same red. If we tried to cheat on this and just get close, we'd kick ourselves every time we walked by the picture on the mantel. To get kids to actually wear these coordinating outfits was another story. Comfortable holiday outfits did not exist for children back then, and they knew it. They also knew they would have to stand and smile then sit and wait then lean and smile then sit and wait then stand and smile again while tilting their head a little...all without getting wrinkled.

And if they were too young to understand, they would just hate the big scary camera.

As excited as we were about these yearly photos, the trip to get there was very stressful and the kids picked up on it. All over the mall, parents dragged their red, white, and green dressed children to the photo shoot, desperately promising all kinds of things along the way. No wonder it was impossible to avoid *the smudge*. Even with only three inches of white turtleneck sticking out or a tiny Peter Pan collar, inevitably, a smudge! Where in the world did it come from? *Maybe walking by that man on the bench eating a burrito? I hope it isn't a mashed chocolate something on the bottom of the stroller.*

Could it have happened when the photographer was positioning the kids on the sleigh? Hmm...so they could charge extra for touch-ups?

After successfully securing the holiday-card photo, it was safe to proceed to the next holiday tradition of visiting Santa. Although Santa also offered a Christmas photo, it was a big mistake to get your card photo there. They'd try to lure people in with a big, beautifully decorated tree surrounded by a sparkling holiday scene. They'd even have a couple of elves running around to add to the experience. But the elves usually had very little photography experience and tried to pawn off blurry pictures for an astronomical price. After all, who can say no to an elf? They also tried, before allowing us to see the picture, to get us to commit to an upgraded package by throwing in a free key chain...rather devious for an elf. The line wrapped around three quarters of the mall, which was heated to 99 degrees, as they seemed to ignore pleas from the Federal Government to conserve energy. But the real problem was, as much as the kids begged to go see old St. Nick every year, someone always got cold feet on the approach. Usually the apprehension set in as we rounded the last bend in the hour-long line and they got their first real glimpse of him. It was hard to believe they'd throw away the chance to ask Santa, in person, for what they wanted to find under the tree. So we'd bring them up to him anyway, thinking once they heard his jolly ol' "Ho ho ho," and saw the twinkle in his eye, they'd have a change of heart. The problem was, most mall Santa's didn't have a twinkle in their eyes and instead looked like they are in desperate need of a nap.

The elves weren't much help either. The only thing they had to offer was shaking a stuffed Rudolph in the kid's face, as though this would suddenly make them roar with laughter.

Indeed, a hysterical child, clawing to get away from jolly old St. Nick, did not illustrate Happy Holidays. The only choice was to hold the screaming, thrashing child, let the elf take a quick picture, and buy one 2"x3" just to get out of there. The photo would understandably go into a drawer somewhere. By the time the younger kids didn't need you to stand in the picture anymore, the older ones didn't believe and stood with nauseated expressions. Basically, the sooner we could convince the kids to just write a letter to Santa, the better off we were.

Of course, we all want to pass our treasured

family traditions on to our children. This process begins with the age-old practice of baking holiday cookies with young children. Honestly, I don't know how traditions make it. First of all, because we've spent so much time perfecting these recipes, they've become sacred to us. Sometimes they even become our signature contribution to gatherings. So to watch children drop egg shells in the batter, over-pour the vanilla and under-beat the butter is heart wrenching. That along with their awkward forming of dough balls and haphazard placement on the cookie sheet, was enough to make you want to pop in the Barney video and boot them out of the kitchen. But instead we swallowed hard and stood by watching our favorite recipes get slaughtered to an unrecognizable state. Will it all pay off? Of course it will, because down the line we'll be thrilled when the kids show up in our nursing homes with our favorite holiday cookies for us. We also learned one of the hardest lessons of parenting...let it go!

Remembering to "let it go" was also helpful

when our kids stopped believing in Santa. Many of us fought this tooth and nail, going to great pains to preserve the image of Santa shooting up and down the chimney. Each year we'd get a little more careful, adding convincing touches to the Christmas morning rituals. "Oh, look," we'd say with sincere amazement, pointing out the footprints we'd trampled in the snow the night before. "Wow," we'd declare with genuine delight, as they discovered Santa's response to their note. The note Dad wrote using his left hand to disguise the handwriting. It was like having a part in a Broadway play every year as we got into character for the role. Until the day came when your child stepped off the bus announcing to your horror, "Larry said there is *no Santa*." Most children find out on the bus. We had to resist the urge to kill Larry and instead, let it go. We had to swallow hard, like with the cookies, and watch another cherished tradition crumble away. Until, of course it was your third child stepping off the bus. Then you wanted to kiss Larry. By number three, the excitement of keeping the Santa secret had just plain fizzled out.

It was time for the play to go off Broadway. We were tired of jumping through all the Santa hoops and ready to embrace everyone being in the know.

Admit it, once the last child stopped believing in Santa, the pressures of the holiday eased up some, allowing us to gain a sense of control. Not that we could control everything. The unexpected was a given around the holidays. For instance, did you ever have one of the kids start throwing up just as you finished dressing for the holiday work party? There you are in your brand new snowman sweater holding a kid's head over the toilet.

Nooo, you were frantically thinking to yourself, not tonight! I'm sure this is going to pass quickly. Could you clean it up and clear the air before the babysitter arrived, and maybe not mention it? Wait a minute. Didn't they have the holiday party in school today? *Yes, that's it! He's not sick. It's all the junk food he ate at the darn party. Didn't he mention he consumed two brownies, four cookies, a cupcake, and five chocolate Santas, with a chaser of candy canes? Of course he's going to throw up!* To go or not to go became the dilemma. Do bad parents go and good parents stay? That was when the fine art of rationalization would save you if you let it. You rationally decided it wouldn't hurt your kid if a sixteen-year-old cleaned up their puke. Besides, it was more likely they'd be running around the house three minutes after you walked out the door, feeling perfectly fine. If you stayed home...keep reading, you're my target audience.

Equally as unanticipated was the lost gift. Hidden away in a "safe place" was the gift you knew you had but when you went to wrap it, was nowhere to be found. How could this happen?! You could visualize it sitting right there, where it wasn't. So you tore the house apart and found the lost gift from last year. This should have been a clue to stop and "let it go," but you didn't. You refused to allow the force of the holidays to win. Not this year! On and on you went, turning the house upside down until there was nowhere else to look. And yup, the force of the holidays won.

The faster we became realistic about the family evening of decorating the tree, the better off we were, as well. I know the Hallmark holiday specials show everyone tenderly removing the precious ornaments from boxes and delicately placing them on the tree. Families are engaged in the moment, sharing pleasant conversation. Maybe sipping a little hot cocoa and nibbling on some gingerbread men. The dog is sleeping by the roaring fire, the cat curled up on the overstuffed chair. Nice...right? Wrong. Because it was more like everyone pushing and shoving to get an ornament out of the cardboard box that was falling apart and collapsing. One or two of the fragile ornaments crashing to the floor from kids colliding or not hanging them on the branch correctly. The husband and teenage boys more engaged in the football game than the tree. The dog picking up on the excitement and running around, knocking the ornaments off the bottom branches, while the cat made her way *into* the tree. And if you were crazy enough to have hot cocoa in the middle of this chaos, it would surely end up on the carpet. Not to mention, you hadn't even gotten close to making gingerbread men yet! Sound more like it? One of the miracles of Christmas to me each year was in spite of it all, when I finally got a minute to stand back and breathe, somehow the tree was amazingly beautiful. As for the broken ornaments, well, they made room in the box for the new ones you'd get as gifts that year, continuing the ornament circle of life.

My very favorite ornaments were, hands down, the picture ornaments the kids made in school. A little less glitter glue might have been good, as they always glitter up the other ornaments, but they're still the winners. How about the gifts the kids bought you on their own from the Secret Santa store at school? How many rings did you get that turned your finger green? Guys, how many pocket-sized tool sets in a plastic car-shaped holder? Sometimes our kids would get the creative teacher who had the kids *make* the gift for their parents. Noodle jewelry was always a favorite with them. I wore a noodle necklace to church one Christmas but the noodles melted from my body heat resulting in my having to peel them off my skin. The decorated pine cone Christmas trees were also a favorite with the crafty teachers. We still have one of those proudly displayed. Sometimes a teacher who was not so crafty would attempt to be crafty, putting us in the difficult position of figuring out what the gift was without hurting our child's feelings. Usually those teachers went with cotton-ball projects resembling a snowman, a reindeer, a Santa, or all of the above. We learned the hard way never to throw out a guess until we were sure.

This may be a *guilt* trigger, but isn't it kind of cool to get real gifts from our kids now? Having them go to a store and spend their own money on a little something for Mom and Dad is a turning point in a parent's life. It is fine to like this, as this book is all about discovering why you deserve things after raising the kids.

Think what you used to go through to find the one thing they really wanted for Christmas. You'd rush to the store before it opened and wait at the door to be one of the first in. Then you'd muscle your way through all the other parents to make sure you got one. There were also the last minute runs out to a store for the pile equalizer gifts, when you noticed one kid's pile was a little smaller than the others. How about the strategic hiding of the gifts then re-hiding when you sensed they were on to you, probably when the lost gift happened.

There was the wrapping it all up, carefully differentiating Santa gifts from parent gifts. And then the setup!

The setup would have been fun if we'd had any energy left to enjoy it. Instead, we were going through the motions in a stupor. I have vague memories of filling stockings, assembling dollhouses, constructing tents, and snapping together all kinds of things well into the night. Taking batteries out of TV remotes, forgetting to buy them for the battery-operated toys, and taking bites out of Santa's cookies, hoping they'd notice. Then, finally, with Mama in her kerchief and Pa in his cap, we'd collapse into bed. Three hours later, the kids woke up. There they stood, at the foot of your bed, screaming at a deafening pitch, "Santa came. Santa came." And awaking with a startle, we thought, Impossible, it can't be morning. But it was, and we sprang into action. It was show time for the big role we'd been preparing to perform for weeks. With the camcorder ready to roll, tree lights on, we announced to the children corralled at the top of the steps, "Ready." Don't get me wrong, I loved Christmas morning with our kids, watching them bound into the room, unable to contain their excitement. Their jubilation as they made their way through their evenly distributed piles, making us glad we persevered to find those sought-after gifts. But as heartwarming as it all was, the exhaustion, a tiredness that permeated deep into our bones, is hard to forget. Adrenalin got us through it, even through the family visits later in the day, but by December 26th, we were *done*! No sane person with children gets dressed the day after Christmas.

The funny thing about kids is the more over stimulated and tired they are, the more energy they expend. If you could bottle a child's December 26th energy, it would need to be regulated by Homeland Security. It's the reason so many Christmas presents don't make it to day two.

Eventually the energy burns off...relief. Then they get the flu. We always blamed that on the relative who showed up sick at the holiday gathering. You know, the one who came and coughed on everyone because they couldn't stand to miss the fun. Really, it was more the kids had hit a debilitating state of exhaustion.

But fun it will be as we proceed to reward ourselves for all the holiday hoopla we've gone through over the years. We could start with making our own holiday wish list for us, yes us. It probably won't be as elaborate as the ones our kids made, numbered in order of priority with the circled advertisements attached. But maybe a nice, simple, somewhat-specific list. It's always an eye-opener for our kids when we mimic their behaviors. Like when we sing along to "their" songs in the car. They hate that! But they could never call us out on a Christmas wish list. Also, it must be hung on the refrigerator. It's tradition.

Good start, but we need more. Remember, Christmas morning redefined exhaustion. Let's work with that. Our kids are now at the age where the early morning hours are not their "fav," right? So we'll wake them up early Christmas morning like they used to wake us. Yes, we can stand at the bottom of their beds, screaming at a deafening pitch "Santa came, Santa came."

If they aren't with you Christmas morning, their phone is never more than six inches from their ear. If you feel you need even more, pictures could be the icing on the fruitcake. Think what they put us through year after year to get those holiday-card pictures. Keep the images of those smudged turtlenecks in your thoughts as you snap away. Best if you can take a few when they've just been shaken out of bed, before they're camera ready, which is also not their "fav." Of course, it's all in good cheer, as that's what the holidays are all about. Of course....

So as we remember the challenges of all the years of holiday hoopla we've been through with our kids, I do hope it brings back some wonderful memories as well. In the end it was all worth it and tons of fun and good cheer, providing us with memories to last a lifetime. We became astutely aware of this...once we recovered.

And did it...

amazingly **Guiltless!**

Chapter Eight
Birthday Party Madness

Birthday parties for our kids were very much like childbirth. The memory of the pain faded over time, so we did it again. We'd swear we were done and then, a year or two later, having forgotten the discomfort, we were right back at it. The party theme discussions began minutes after we gave the go-ahead for a party, because it was always all about the party theme. Luckily for us, Disney movies monopolized our children's generation of party themes, so party supplies were readily available. Two hundred and fifty dollars later, we staggered out of the store ready to celebrate our child's turning another year older.

Did you ever wonder why such a huge emphasis was put on turning another year older in life? Why did it turn into such an extravaganza? Maybe we got this all wrong.

Maybe it should be like a quick turn of the

calendar and on we go. No different than moving from July to August...expected. No different than the leaves changing in the fall or the tulips popping up in spring...just expected. Maybe it would have given our kids a different sense of their place on earth and life's expectations in general. Although I think we all know...Disney would never have allowed it.

So, on with the party! My husband always felt he could handle the entertainment himself, as he had a lot of experience working with kids in a camp setting. He'd pull out his best material, all the old favorites. With his famous "Herman the Worm" story, he was ready to wow the crowd. Somehow, this played out better in our minds than in real time. Even his attempts to involve audience participation, which had always worked in the 1980s, resulted in blank stares. The "Night Walk" was another favorite, where he'd have the kids walk around the yard in the pitch dark without flashlights, relying on their night vision to explore the outdoors. He'd try his best to sell it, "Come on, you guys," he would plead, "this is really fun." Still, it did not seem to pack the same punch as in our day. Turned out the kids couldn't see crap with their night vision, and most of them ended up falling into the hedges bordering the yard. They seemed more interested in getting back to entertaining themselves by destroying our house.

Until we brought out the ice cream cake. If there's one lesson I learned from our kids' birthday parties over the years, it would be to bag the ice cream cake. When parents try to serve ice cream cake at a child's birthday party, they are working against too many laws of physics. The *factors affecting melting points* become a real problem. By the time the parent has gathered the kids around the table, passed out the party hats, replaced the ones the elastic snapped on, gotten ice for the kid whose elastic snapped, lit the candles, relit the ones the older brother blew out, sung the song, really blown out the candles, and run to the freezer to grab a popsicle for the kid who's announced he's lactose intolerant...instead of cake, you had soup! So much for serving it in your carefully selected party-themed cake plates, you were looking for cereal bowls, and who had more than six of those? Tupperware was always the backup and once the kids discovered the lids could make them burp, you had a whole new party theme going. I remember vividly how quickly the theme of our son's eighth birthday party changed from Power Rangers to burping after the ice cream cake.

That led right into burping contests which, to be honest, helped with the entertainment portion of the afternoon. That party is actually still talked about when the kids sit around reminiscing...it's legendary.

Usually gift opening followed the cake. That's when parents discovered their child told every one of their friends what they wanted for their birthday, and their friends got it. There lay four of the same Spaceship Lego Sets or Summer Fun Barbie Dolls, amongst the appropriately themed wrapping paper. If we'd resisted regifting up to this point in our life, it was a guarantee we'd cave now. It was just too easy to stash away one of the four identical Polly Pockets for the cousin in Massachusetts' next birthday. Younger siblings thought they would make out in this scenario, but the birthday children were way too aware of the birthday rule. It was their day and brothers and sisters had to deal with it. As expected, this created a problem with siblings, as they never bought that rule. Also, the younger ones constantly tried to keep up with the cool big kids...and couldn't. And the older ones wanted to show off for the little kids...and could. All these birthday party scenarios together would generally drive the birthday child crazy.

There were many ways of handling this. Some tried locking siblings away in another area of the house, which was fine with the right kind of awesome snacks set up to keep them there. Others tried relocating them off site. We preferred to go with survival of the fittest with the younger kids and the power trip method for the older ones. Survival of the fittest would usually result in the younger kids retreating to another area of the house in defeat, not even caring whether there were awesome snacks. But allowing the older ones to be responsible for a job could really work. It played right into their power-hungry egos, with the added benefit of an extra set of hands. As long as we closely monitored the bullying potential with this, it usually ended up a good thing. Giving them the job of guarding the goody bags was perfect, as we really needed a heavy hitter to handle that.

Goody bags were a key component to our kids' birthday parties. Once we realized this, we could use them to our advantage in addressing behaviors during the party. All we had to do was threaten withholding a goody bag, and even the kid organizing a sliding-down-the-banister contest would rethink his actions. This was surprising, considering these goody bags were nothing more than a bunch of cheap plastic toys and dried-up penny candy in an overpriced Disney-themed bag. We could put almost anything in those bags and kids would love it. I only goofed up once when I foolishly put mini

Super Balls in it. I don't know what I was thinking. That resulted in twelve Super Balls ricocheting all over our family room while the kids were waiting for their parents to arrive. Also, no matter where we hid the goody bags during the birthday party, we ran the risk of someone discovering them prematurely. Nothing dismantles a birthday party faster than a kid surfacing with a goody bag in the middle of the party and revealing its contents to the other kids. If this happened, a quick response was needed to prevent *goody bag distribution sabotage*. This happened at one of our parties, when the older sibling left their post, but I was able to quickly confiscate them and turn the ill-fated moment around with a movie.

Movies were lifesavers at children's birthday parties. A parent could easily kill two hours with a good movie if necessary. We could also successfully tuck younger siblings, who had resurfaced, into the corner of the room as stowaways, and they would not be noticed. Movies were great as long as we were very selective. None of us wanted to give the birthday party that provided all the eight-year-olds in the neighborhood with their first sex-ed lesson. It was always best to leave such things to the bus. Let's face it, the school bus rides were the main informant of our children's sex education. Parents' attempts to explain the subject could not compare. I really don't know what the walkers did. Anyway, too much violence in a movie could be a showstopper, so we couldn't listen to our kid's suggestion, which was guaranteed to have violence. We didn't always use a movie at our parties, but we always had one ready in the wings for party emergencies.

Sometimes a child actually had an imagination and came up with their own unique idea for a party theme. Yes, a kid who thought outside the Disney-themed box. If we had a kid with their own party-theme idea, like frogs on lily pads or soaring spaceships, well, we had our work cut out for us. Chances are it would be impossible to find a line of plates, napkins, cups, tablecloth, Piñata, balloons, and centerpiece for their idea. This was a tough position to be in. If word got out the party was a hodgepodge combination, it would be the topic of conversation after the next PTA meeting. Birthday party themes held a higher importance in our generation of parenting than what age the child was turning. People didn't ask, "How old are you going to be?" Nope, the question was, "What's your Disney birthday theme?" It wasn't easy to change a kid's mind once they locked their heart and soul around a party theme. We could offer them the world and those stubborn little feet would remain planted, arms crossed, with a stare that could crumble the Great Wall of China. The only way to redirect a kid's mind away from a non-Disney, birthday party theme was to outsource. In other words, take the show on the road!

Luckily, there were some very good choices available to us for outsourcing our children's birthday parties. One option was the fast-food chain with a big enclosed playscape and a pit of plastic balls to dive in. I often regretted not thinking this idea up myself. It couldn't be simpler, hollow plastic balls kids could safely jump into. They could bury themselves without suffocating and even throw them at each other without causing injury. This genius idea allowed fast-food chains to delve into the thriving market of children's birthday parties. They would even throw in an employee to run the party. These employees were usually low-energy, expressionless seventeen-year-olds who spoke in a monotone voice, making it very clear they'd rather be anywhere but doing your party. The kids, however, didn't seem to notice and it still took a lot of the party burden off our shoulders. Not a bad deal for the parent and a definite win in getting your kid to drop their non-Disney theme. For girls, you also had the popular choice of the beauty shop. At first I couldn't believe a beauty shop would want to take this on. But they did, and there you'd sit, watching a group of eight-year-olds getting updos, makeup, and manicures. The girls absolutely loved this, but there were some pretty shocked looks on parents' faces when they picked up their innocent little girls looking like they were ready for the red-light district. Outsourcing our children's birthday parties also moved the shock and awe of destruction out of our house.

No mashed cake in the carpet or pizza crusts under the couch. The potted plants remained in their pots, and we could walk through our house without your shoes sticking to the floor when the party was over.

This option for our kids' birthday parties was not completely stress free. We did have to consider the very high risk of losing kids when hitting the road with a group of party goers. Especially places like Chuck E. Cheese's that were not only crowded and spread out, but so noisy we could barely think straight. After an hour you could barely remember why you were there, let alone who was there. You couldn't keep track of kids in a place like Chuck E. Cheese's if your life depended on it, and it did. It was a real problem if you greeted a parent with a blank, quizzical stare when they arrived to pick up their child. "Oh, you're here for your child Sammy," while desperately trying to remember who the heck Sammy was. It was better for everyone involved if you just faked it and took a stab. "He's over by the pinball machine," knowing full well you didn't have a clue if he was. If wrong, we could always begin the goody bag distribution. Once word of this got out, the party goers would come flocking from every corner of Chuck E. Cheese's, and Sammy was guaranteed to surface.

Sometimes our kids badgered us into having a sleepover birthday party. Sleepover birthday parties brought us right back to the shock and awe destruction of our home, as well as our mind, body, and soul. Torturous is the only word that comes to mind for sleepover birthday parties, considering how long it had been since most parents had been up for an all-nighter. Even knowing our staying up all night was no longer an option, we still agreed to this. Did we think the kids would actually lay their over stimulated little heads on their pillows and nicely slip into peaceful slumber? Did we think even if they didn't, we could go to bed and they would talk nicely amongst themselves until they drifted off to sleep? When forty-something-year-olds stay up all night for a child's birthday party they transform into another life form. Their facial expressions, voices, stance, and gait all become unrecognizable. So when that person, or thing, stands at the top of the stairs at three o'clock in the morning, desperately pleading for everyone to stop wrestling and go to sleep, it's quite a shock for the neighborhood kids. Even our own kids didn't recognize us. It didn't take long for the pleading to turn into a bellow of "That's it. I've had it. Go to sleep...now!" At that point we didn't care what the kids, their parents, or the PTA thought about the party.

As soon as the last kid left, the last party-themed plate thrown away, the piñata pieces swept away, and three of the four same Nerf guns were confiscated to regift...the phone rang. There it was, the call from your mother-in-law, asking when we're having the family birthday party. Not even finished licking the wounds from the kid party, we are now expected to have thirty-five immediate family members over to our ranch starter house to celebrate the already thoroughly acknowledged existence of our child. Ducking out of this part of life's expected family ritual is impossible, not that I didn't try. Some family members would wait with bated breath all year long for this event. They are the ones who showed up with the flashing helmet with a built-in siren as a gift for your son, and laughed themselves silly as he ran around the house with it, causing the cat to have a seizure. They are the ones who would slip the child candy before dinner, soda with caffeine, and a second piece of cake, again laughing away at the child's sugar high. They are also notorious for spinning the child around by their arms, while you wait for their sockets to pop, dangling them upside down, or tickling them till they can't breathe then, you guessed it, laughing their heads off. Don't get me wrong. I feel family bonding is a very important part of a child's upbringing and fosters valuable lifelong relationships, just not back to back with a kid's friend's birthday party!

Doing a family party first didn't work either, because of the enormous amount of deprogramming your child required afterwards, as well as dietary cleansing. It took days to get their blood sugar down to a level where they could speak at a normal volume, focusing on one thought at a time. It took weeks to get them to stop balancing spoons on their nose at dinner and flipping their eyelids inside out, tricks learned from the older cousins. And it took a good month before they stopped repeating the dirty jokes they overheard the uncles telling. Not to mention, between the kid party and the family party, the child has now received more toys than a community toy drive. We actually created a "bored" closet as a result of this inundation of new toys from birthday parties.

The presents that we didn't regift, we tucked away in our "bored" closet in the back basement and rotated them out. This definitely goes down as one of our family's better parenting ideas over the years. Believe it or not, that closet is still filled with old favorites.

Come on, we all had certain toys we couldn't part with. Who doesn't still have a box of dinosaurs or a Playschool school bus tucked away somewhere? Can't hurt to save them for the grandchildren.

Grandchildren will be the ticket to rewarding ourselves for the tortures we went through with our kids' birthday parties. It's just too easy. We'll be the relatives who wait all year to come to *their* house. We'll be the ones to call the minute the last guest leaves our grandchild's kid party and ask our kids when *they* are having the family party. We can buy all the noisy, obnoxious gifts they won't buy *their* children, and laugh ourselves silly when our grandchildren run around the house out of control. Hey, I have a good one...we can whisper a non-Disney party theme in our grandchild's ear a month before their birthday. This must be why people say grandchildren are so much more fun than raising your own.

I suppose if we are going to cash in with such

vengeance, we should balance it, or disguise it, with loving gestures. After all, as grandparents we'll have a reputation to uphold. So when our kids call us disgusted they had to serve their ice cream cake with straws, had to Google what the kid with a gluten allergy can eat, and how they had to patch another kid's eye from a party hat snapping...we should reply with empathy. When they describe the shattered lamp, the juice stain on their carpet, and the dead fish in the tank...we should sigh heavily and sympathize. And when they pull out their hair as their child is doing cartwheels through the house from the overstimulation of the family party...we should show sincere compassion.

But in the end, after all that empathy, sympathy, and compassion are expressed lovingly from the bottom of my heart, I am here to tell you...I'll be laughing myself silly!

And doing it...

amazingly Guiltless!

Chapter Nine
Shopping Shenanigans

If you're wondering why I wrote about shopping with kids, then you must have blocked this experience from your memory. It's okay, just keep reading, and the terror will soon creep back into your memory, evident by an increase in heart rate and clenching of your throat. No, you're not having a heart attack. You're simply remembering all the shenanigans of shopping with your kids.

The child rearing books, once again, tell us this is a great opportunity to bond with our child. At this point parents start to realize the people writing these books clearly have never raised a kid, and start using their books to prop up wobbly table legs. Let's review why the bonding-by-shopping theory was so full of hot air. First of all, we strapped them into a stroller and wheeled them around with their eyes at kneecap height, not seeing their angelic little faces unless they leaned out headed for a face plant. Then, we secured toys inside their strollers to keep them busy so they wouldn't bother us. We provided a constant flow of refreshments, again so they would not interrupt us. Our attention was focused on juggling shopping bags, the diaper bag, a purse and, of course, coupons. Today's poor parents have to add a cell phone to the list, thank goodness we didn't have that burden. In addition, there was the tedious searching for sizes, color choice, and calculating 20 percent off. Point is, we were giving very little attention to our kids when shopping with them. There was also the race against the clock to accomplish what we absolutely had to get done before the shopping meltdown.

Nothing brought an end to our trip like the shopping meltdown. Surprisingly, young children do not like to shop. Wouldn't you think getting to ride around a store with so many new and interesting things to look at would be fun for a kid? The elaborate displays, piped-in music, and bright lights...how could that not be entertaining? Was the minimally padded stroller with a 90 degree upright seat not comfortable enough? Remember, we didn't have the ergonomically correct, breathable, cushioned seats available today. Our poor kids were stuck with the sub-standard equipment of the 1980s, or even 1970s if it was a hand-me-down. Maybe the fluorescent lighting irritated their central nervous systems? I suppose it's scientifically possible. Or maybe it was those little old ladies making a fuss over them at every turn, undeniably invading their social bubble. Those old ladies practically attacked kids, tousling their hair, pinching their cheeks, and squeezing their chubby little arms. Whatever the reason, shopping meltdowns were intense. The sounds that came out of a child could dub as a soundtrack for horror movies, as their angelic little faces became monster-like. How they managed to contort their bodies like that is still a mystery to me. They'd go into a full-body collapse, with every ligament and muscle becoming completely pliable. We'd swear they were covered with petroleum jelly as they slipped through our arms. You tripled them in height and weight, but somehow they were winning the struggle. Forget about distracting them with the puppies at the pet store or pacifying them with an ice cream, there was no consoling a shopping meltdown. Our only recourse was to beeline it to the door, dodging as many little old lady accusatory looks as possible. We had to get them into the car and home as fast as we could. If you were lucky they would scream themselves to sleep in the car, but most times they just screamed. We were exhausted and drenched in sweat by the time we got home. Once in the door, and into dry clothes, attempting to do anything else for the rest of the day was absolutely out of the question.

But we had no choice! We couldn't hire a sitter every time we needed to step into a store. Without a live-in nanny, those kids were coming with us. My mother always said, "Necessity is the mother of invention," so out of necessity we figured out how to make this work. It became routine to grab water bottles and granola bars when walking out the door. I never bought a handbag that couldn't accommodate three servings of each, a *mission-control purse* as I called it. I'd marvel at the women walking around with stylish little handbags and wondered what kind of life they must have? Would I ever get to a point in life when I could operate with one of those? The answer is no. When you do this for so many years it becomes impossible to leave the house without granola bars and water stashed in your purse. A feeling of helplessness and panic sets in if you do. Even long after the kids are out of the house, I'm still stashing. My twenty-year-olds marvel each time I pull these supplies out of my purse. "Mom," they moan, "we aren't going to outer Mongolia." Still, I'm ready.

Thinking back, our kids really were captured in those strollers with no control over where we dragged them. Poor things didn't even have control over what they could touch, as we barked "don't touch" every time they reached out for anything. I wonder if we should have worked in a little freedom along the way. I'm not saying we should have let them run freely like the oblivious parents did. The ones with their kids wandering half a mile behind them, pulling items off displays and picking up gummy bears dropped by the kid in the stroller. Those oblivious parents would shop without strollers, without entertainment, and even without snacks.

What were they thinking?! It was an insult to those of us who worked so hard to master the process. How could they just show up in a store, kids in tow, and wing it? The only consolation would be hearing them paged to the front of the store when their kid was found peeking under the doors in the ladies' dressing room. Still, they'd nonchalantly collect their offspring from store security and continue on, all loosey goosey about the whole thing, never breaking a sweat.

Unfortunately, even the most conscientious of us experienced an occasional moment of losing sight of our child in a store. The feeling of panic when this happened was comparable to the first 10 seconds of bungee jumping. A palpable leap of the heart, coiling of the stomach, and total collapse of our cranium. Sure we were never going to see your child again, we were blind to anything in our path as we tore through the store searching for them. Seconds felt like hours, minutes felt like days, and then we found them. Sitting under the 25 percent sale rack, two feet away. Okay, yes, eating some kid's dropped gummy bears. Even though your child was only out of sight for thirty to forty seconds, we felt sickened and confidence in our ability to parent was shaken. We'd go over and over it in our head until it hit us. Of course, that's it, you were going through the 75 percent off rack! It all made sense now. Nobody can be expected to keep their wits about them at a 75 percent off rack!

As our kids got older, we foolishly thought shopping with them would get easier. We figured not having to deal with strollers or lug around entertainment would make shopping with them a breeze. Wrong! We forgot to consider their newly heightened awareness of available products, and the impact it would have on a shopping trip. "You want what?" "What do you mean everyone else has one?" There was a desperation and intenseness with these conversations we hadn't seen in them since the terrible twos. It was as if the world would dissolve around them if they didn't get that pair of pants, in that brand, from that store with the blaring music. Even though we'd just seen an identical pair of pants, in another brand, from another store, for half the price. Basically, if they got the imposter, life as they knew it would be over. Eventually, their dramatic display of emotion started to effect the decision-making area of our gray matter, persuading us to throw them a lifeline. Were they attending marketing courses in middle school? We teetered between believing them and ruining their lives. I guess we all have adolescent memories of when we showed up with the knockoff of what was in style and...well, let's just say, we do still remember. Were we setting our kid up for that? "Okay, okay we'll get it *this* time," we said in a stern voice so they didn't expect us to give in every time. As much as we set out on each shopping trip thinking we wouldn't cave to the brand-name monster, we *are* called the kid-pleaser generation for a reason.

Our only recourse was to continue the age-old practice of pinching their toes when trying on shoes. Also, the finger test on the collar and the waistband tug.

These rituals have been passed down from generation to generation and provide parents a means of getting back at their kids for all they put them through when shopping. These practices would cause considerable dismay with our kids especially around the middle school years. Boy, I hope you never got caught tugging a waistband when your kids' friend walked by. If so, you could rewind back to shopping meltdown times ten, with their faces becoming monster-like and indescribable noises coming out of their mouths. This was another shopping showstopper followed by another unpleasant trip home. For parents, it was all about assuring the clothing would fit for more than two months, but for the kids it was embarrassing parent stuff. This is one of those things that won't make sense to them until they are pinching and tugging their own kids' pants...and they will.

Shopping with high school kids was never a problem. They just outright wouldn't do it. Instead they took the money, came home with things we didn't approve of, and lost the receipts. That is, once we trained them to navigate a mall independently. Training your child to operate alone in the mall was a process and usually began with the "fade back." We'd drive them and their most responsible-looking friend to the mall, reviewing mall safety procedures on the way. This resulted in a lot of eye rolling and sighs from our child and the friend. Once in the mall, we'd synchronize our watches with theirs and agree on a meeting plan. We would then check cell phone charges, offer another quick reminder of "don't do drugs" then separate with the understanding you would remain in the mall in case they needed you. We knew there would have to be an apocalyptic event for them to need you, but whatever.

As we're walking away, we start to rethink the plan. *Is this really a good idea? Am I being a responsible parent?* All of a sudden, everyone we pass looks like they've escaped from a penitentiary. Where did all these hoodlums come from? *And where are the security guards? Isn't there supposed to be security in malls? Did I tell them that?* It's only been twenty minutes, but an innocent little check wouldn't hurt. We start scanning the crowd over the banister from the second level. No sign of them. A glimpse would calm our uneasiness, so we moved on to the lower level. More hoodlums. Was that a cross and skull on his arm? That's it, we call, no answer. Call again, no answer. Now we're speed walking through the mall, and people are staring at you as if concerned something is very wrong. In and out of the stores we march with no sign of them.

Finally, as we're reaching a state of desperation with still no security in sight, there they are sitting at the food court sipping a soda. We approach them, coat flapping, hair flying, eyes bugging out of our head. They look at us like we're insane, and we look at them amazed they haven't been stuffed into the trunk of the car of the guy we just passed with five chin piercings. Exasperated, we plop down next to them, even though that's not allowed, take a sip of their soda to recover, and quickly inform them about the security guards available. They again head off on their own after more eye rolling, sighs, and this time an added look of disgust. Each time this gets a little easier until they, really you, get to the point that they're, really you're, comfortable. Preparing kids to be independent at the mall is a grueling process that ends when they wear you down to a pulp and you have no strength left to worry...so you pretend you're comfortable.

Funny how once they go to college, all of a sudden they *want* to shop with us. They quickly pick up on how our missing them results in our buying them stuff. It's our parental instinct to make sure they have what they need to be comfy when we're not there with them. Our parents' generation didn't have that instinct because I remember having to use whatever I could find around the house to get comfy. So even though we knew they were taking advantage of our fragile state of mind, we did this. I found myself buying them things we didn't even have at home. They'd get a nice new set of matching towels, while we were trimming loose threads from ours. They'd get a cushioned pad for their desk chair, while we were sitting on hard wood. A new this, a new that. It was like a bridal shower every August. The only thing that saved our particular family was brainwashing our kids early on about *on sale*. From the time our children could sit up in the basket of the shopping cart, they thought the only items you could purchase were those marked on sale. I guess our consistent response of, "No, we'll wait till it's *on sale*" penetrated their impressionable little minds. So, to this day, they still go right to the sale racks. Nice when we can score a win without any conscious effort. Once when our daughter was four she was shopping with Grandma, and went into a full-fledged panic attack when Grandma reached for something that was not marked on sale. She accused her grandmother of shoplifting and cried all the way home. This may be something they'll need to tell a therapist about someday, but until then it's on sale or no sale!

So now for our reward for all the shenanigans we've been through when shopping with our kids. Solo shopping!

It's the thing you used to fit in between kid activities, or sneak out to do in the evening after arranging for meals, homework, and baths. Well, it's now yours for the taking. A world of shopping where you can think clearly and weigh options. No strollers or shopping entertainment to worry about, just *you*. How wonderful to walk freely from rack to rack without having to sustain another life form.

Remember the juggling act you used to go through to purchase a birthday card or do a quick return? Usually returning the item you bought when you couldn't think straight from a kid begging you to leave.

So let's do this! Who cares if we can't find what we want right away. There's no need to work against the clock in fear of a shopping meltdown. We can browse all we want, as we have earned our place at the pearly gates of shopping heaven.

Once you really master solo shopping, you'll be looked at as a kind of professional. People will come up to you and ask shopping questions. This happens to me all the time now. Things like, "Can you tell me where to find the coffee makers," or "Have you ever tried this mouthwash?" This means you have thoroughly mastered the solo-shopping experience as well as the strut of delightful freedom.

There is another level we could take this to where we could really celebrate our freedom. We could plan a weekend outing to the outlets with some friends. Although many men shop, they don't usually want to take it to this level. But if you're in, think of how amazing it would be to have an entire weekend of uninterrupted retailing, with adults who can look after themselves at the 75 percent off rack. Actual human beings who you can collaborate with, discuss purchases, and who can handle their own water bottles. This is shopping at its finest! There is nothing more rewarding than throwing yourself into the hands of retailers for endless hours, allowing yourself to be swept away. We could even leave our *mission-control purse* behind, and bring a little stylish handbag just big enough for our wallet and coupons. This is our chance to be one of *those* women! Don't look left, don't look right; let the retail forces guide you.

We're entering a whole new wonderful world of shopping possibilities. What a perfect reward for all we've gone through over the years, while shopping with our kids. So enjoy!

And do it...

amazingly Guiltless!

Chapter Ten
Playdates

Our generation of parents did not allow our children to just walk out the door and find something to do. We needed to bring them together in a supervised, controlled atmosphere, to enjoy each other's company. Mainly because we are the first generation of parents to raise kids with minute-by-minute news coverage of all the awful things happening in the world. This barrage of worrisome information scared us out of allowing our kids to freely explore the wonders of the world, or even the block. Thanks to the news, we were afraid for our kids to jump on their bikes in the morning, pop in the door for lunch, and then back again for dinner, like we did as kids. Actually, we weren't even allowed back in the door until dinner. "Get out from under my feet," our parents would shout, and shoo us out the door. "The world has changed," we rationalized. "It's not like it was when we were growing up." End result...the playdate was born.

Dramatic reporting by news media gave parents the illusion of danger at every turn. To be fair, it wasn't only the news media; milk cartons were also to blame. When they started to put missing children's pictures on milk cartons, parents felt they could no longer take their eyes off their kids. We needed to know where they were every moment, and what they were doing while there. Playdates were the perfect solution. They took place in our homes, and we had to watch them closely because they involved other people's kids. Our generation of parents took being responsible for another kid very seriously, since any mishap could seriously ruin our playdate-hosting reputation.

Watching kids closely was not always easy. Our one son and his friend went an entire summer in camouflage.

They wore authentic army fatigues an uncle sent from his service in Iraq and were undetectable all day long. If not for an occasional rustle of leaves in the woods beside our house, and the dog blowing their cover, it would have been impossible to check on them. I'd leave sandwiches outside on the picnic table for lunch and knew they were okay when the sandwiches disappeared. I don't even remember bathroom visits now that I think about it, but then again I'd rather not think about it. The only thing that would flush them out of those woods was the ice cream truck. Barreling out of the woods they would come, toy guns flailing and helmets rolling when they heard the whimsical songs from the truck. Camouflage or not, they were not going to miss out on ice cream. Of course, our kids knew they would only get something from the ice cream man on Fridays. Kid-pleaser generation or not, I was not going to make the ice cream man wealthy.

Before arranging a playdate, parents would check a few things out. We all had some sort of screening process. For those with the right connections, fingerprints and drug testing were involved. But most of us had to rely on word of mouth. Along with an informal reference from the PTA, which actually held more weight than the drug test. I once had a close call and almost sent my daughter on a playdate to a home that didn't return four of the last five PTA fundraisers back to the school. Don't want to mess with that kind of poor judgment. We also took into consideration the home's curb appeal. It wasn't ostentation or splendor we were looking for, it was a fence. Fenced-in yards earned extra points, as well as cul-de-sacs. A busy street with no fence scored very low in the screening process.

But even with a perfect score, there was still no guarantee the child was going to work out. We never knew for sure what we were getting into until they got to our house. For us, playdate kids fell into one of the following categories:

The Keepers: Said please and thank you, did not barrage us with questions about our personal life, all Barbie doll shoes matched up afterwards, all Ninja Turtle limbs remained intact, no drink spillage, and ate what we gave them.

Has Potential/Gets a 2nd Chance: Only thanked us for the dessert, only asked, "Where do you see yourself in five years?" lost Barbie Doll shoes we later found in a vase, wanted to watch a movie instead of playing Ninja Turtles. One drink spill, but still ate what we gave them.

Never Ever Coming Back: Walked in with the attitude *nice for you to get to meet me*, interrogated us about our retirement investments, thought Barbie Dolls were dumb, and wanted to play dress up in *our* closet, turned our kid's bunk bed into a live Ninja Turtle game with a pulley rope system to transport items to the top bunk, spilled their drink from the pulley system, and fed their lunch to the dog.

We could ask any parent for an opinion on a kid's playdate category, and be guaranteed to get an honest answer. We all knew we had to stick together on this.

Parents also came together on the fundamental guidelines of playdates. One agreed-upon guideline was to use the guest kid as a bad example if the opportunity presented itself. I know, not the most ethical practice, but if it was dangling right in front of us, we had to take advantage.

For instance, there was the day my son's playdate showed up with a pierced ear. I was shocked he was allowed to do this as an eight-year-old and worried my son would want to copy. So, as they were playing hockey in the driveway and the earring happened to get caught in the goalie net, I went for it. Come on, it was dangling right in front of me. I raced to the scene, knowing I had the entire driveway of kids' undivided attention. "Let's see," I said with what I hoped was a convincing tone of concern. "I don't want to rip the ear lobe too badly," knowing I could easily slip the thing out but also knowing I had to make the most of this golden opportunity. Then, somewhere between one kid's hysterical sobbing and another flagging down the ice cream man for help, I released the ear. This incident held off all piercings on our boys till freshman year of college. What a win!

Another agreed-upon guideline was which

rooms of the house were off-limits for play. In most homes, it included the master bedroom, the parents' safe haven. No toys, no Bernstein Bears books, just our stuff, including a few fragile keepsakes that would never survive the rest of the house. The only children's faces seen there were the smiles beaming from the framed two-year-old pictures on the wall. Okay, some baskets of laundry we hadn't gotten to and a paperwork project in the corner, but it was still a sanctuary...no kids allowed. Some people tried to use a formal living room for this purpose. That rarely worked, and usually involved putting up gates for eighteen years. Kids who lived in homes without a no-kids room would get confused with this kind of restrictive environment. Hence, the occasional child found hiding under your bed. "Shhh, Mrs. S., don't tell him I'm here," they'd whisper when I walked in to fold laundry, "I have a great spot for hide and seek." Well, we couldn't deny them that, as our kids knew they weren't allowed to hide in our bedroom and therefore would never look there. So, as this kid is crushing our wrapping-paper rolls and scratching the leaf to our dining room table, we were in a dilemma on how to handle this. If we blew their cover and ruined their potential hide and seek win, we'd probably get a bad review on their playdate experience at our house. There went your reputation as a playdate host, and word of that would spread like wild fire. But if we let them stay, we had to explain to our kids why their classmate can hide in your bedroom and they can't. Let's face it, the familiar and loving relationship we have with our children works to their disadvantage at times. So the classmate wins hide-and-seek and our kid throws a shoe at him for cheating. There was only one thing that would turn a playdate moment like this around, "Anyone want a snack?"

Having a snack ready at a moment's notice could be a real lifesaver. Nothing broke the "he did it," "she did it" merry-go-round like a good snack. I always asked about food likes and dislikes in my playdate-screening questionnaire. It made for a very long day if the kid hated everything we had to eat in the house, or their face blew up like a balloon from an allergy. Snacks were also the first question parents asked about on the car ride home. Nailing the snack earned major brownie points. It was also the perfect way to pave over the things that hadn't gone so well during the playdate. For example, if your kid actually hit them with a shoe and they were going home with a huge shiner. My favorite playdate snack was the banana boat. This was a banana wrapped in a peanut-butter-covered piece of bread, with stick pretzels poking through it resembling oars. Other than the one kid who thought it looked like a giant centipede and was afraid to touch it, the rest loved it. I was always sure my banana boat racked up major points when being reported to the parent on the ride home. Healthy and fun...major points indeed.

In asking how the playdate went, a parent sometimes learned of happenings clearly against the agreed-upon playdate guidelines. People do like to push the envelope. Sometimes what we learned would even influence whether we would allow our child to play there again. For instance, one mother allowed our daughter to drive a battery-operated car to the end of our street as far as the horse farm, way out of sight of supervision. That definitely was outside the guidelines. Her report on the sugary snack, followed by a sugary soda, followed by an entire bag of chips, put the final nail in the coffin. We highlighted the incident in the final-comment section of their evaluation form. Basically, their playdate reputation was toast.

If things really got shaky, the best way to abort a bad playdate was to offer to drop off the child before the agreed-upon pick-up time. "No problem," we assured their parents. "No trouble at all. I can bring them home on my way to get milk." With a gallon of milk in the refrigerator, we'd drive half way across town, in the pouring rain, listening to the kids' radio station, but it was worth it. The never-coming-back kid was secured with a seat belt in the backseat of the car instead of turning your life upside down. No parent in their right mind would turn down a drop-off offer, so it was a sure-fire plan. Now if our kid ended up raving about the kid we booted off the list, we had to quickly click into parental-excuse mode. This involved the fine art of making it up as we went along. Coming up with those off-the-cuff excuses was one of the biggest challenges of parenting. Kids were amazingly good at countering this. We had to show up with real game to win these challenges and sometimes we didn't. Sometimes we had to endure a second playdate with a kid we didn't like. They couldn't wait to come back, and our kid couldn't wait to have them. Darn those banana boats! However, we did, at some point, have the option to pull rank. After parental excuses came the old standby, parental clout. "No because I said so."

Maybe you even threw in, "Because I can't *stand* the kid." And that was okay.

I guess one of our greatest incentives to endure all this was our desperate attempt to prevent the dreaded state of boredom. Somewhere along the line, it became unacceptable for a kid to wander around looking for something to do. Our kids had ten times the toys we had growing up, twenty times the TV shows, VCRs, and video games, but, somehow, boredom was still a concern. The parents' self-help books, which were now propping up table legs, claimed keeping kids busy was important for stimulating their creativity. I always wonder how providing constant entertainment stimulated creativity more than having them think up something to do on their own.

Regardless, the Kool-Aid commercials also had something to do with this. We were influenced by those nice Kool-Aid moms patiently pouring glass after glass of the popular drink. With sweet, smiling faces these moms would thrill the crowd of youngsters gathered around the picnic table covered with a red-checkered tablecloth. It was a beautiful, sunny summer day, and the kids were in an orderly line nicely waiting for their turn to be handed a cup of the cool beverage. We should have seen right through it, but instead we felt pressured to *be* the Kool-Aid mom. We wanted to experience the same joy of sharing a special moment like this with our kids and their friends. It wasn't until we actually gathered them around our own picnic tables that we learned the real deal. First of all, kids don't stand in nice, orderly lines while waiting for their turn to be handed anything. Also, there isn't a picnic table on earth able to steady cups of Kool-Aid when being barraged by a mob of thirsty eight-year-olds. And don't forget the family dogs that always picked up on the excitement, their wildly wagging tails not only taking out any remaining cups of Kool-Aid, but a couple of kids as well. A gentle, smiling face through all this was out of the question, and that actress mom should have been a shoe-in for an Emmy. Read the package and you discover the Kool-Aid had so much sugar in it one glass made the kids crazy for the rest of the day. Hence, the juice box was born. Hallelujah.

Then there were the teenage years where kids' playdates evolved to actual dates with the opposite sex. This made all the preceding issues, literally, seem like child's play. Forget a supervised, controlled atmosphere. They'd walk in and politely introduce their "friend," and the next thing we knew they were heading down to the basement to watch a movie. Bad idea remodeling it into a nice family room, we should have left it an uninviting dump. Meanwhile, we don't even know this kid; no PTA reference or screening has been done.

A pantry or wood shop down there gave us a reason to go down and check up on things.

"Man oh man, am I ever dying for a snack," grabbing the bag of pretzels while trying to glance into the room darkened for better movie viewing.

"Wow, the stairwell banister is really loose," grabbing the hammer from the work bench while zeroing in on hand placement.

The creaking sound of opening and closing the door at the top of the steps would also put them on alert, in case we ran out of things to fix or eat. On one trip downstairs to get a bag of chips, we discovered our son and his date had opened the sofa bed and sprawled out on it to watch a movie. *Whoa!* I was so taken aback, I came up with canned soup instead of the chips. We immediately called our son upstairs to address this. He calmly and confidently explained to us that it was just *more comfortable*. We not so calmly, but very confidently, suggested he get *uncomfortable*. No amount of disgusted eye rolling could make us feel even a twinge of guilt about this one. Nor were we worried about getting a bad review for this playdate. Surely she wouldn't complain to her parents on the car ride home about not being allowed to lie in a sofa bed with our son to watch a movie.

Besides, she barely made the *has potential* category at that point.

We were advised by the PTA it was better to encourage teenagers to have a group of their friends visit our home, which eliminated the one-on-one scenario. They also advised us to collect coats at the door to stop any smuggling in of alcohol, and to keep track of who was there. All this just to keep our teenager entertained!

Regardless, we arranged the evening stationing one parent at the door to greet the kids and take their coats. Problem was, the second kid who arrived said she was cold and asked to keep her coat on. Now what do we do, let the kid freeze? At that point the only thing left to do was sit on the couch, strain our ears, and worry we would be arrested for allowing underage drinking. We also decided we'd be perfectly fine with the one-on-one scenario from here on out.

The first thing coming to mind when I think about how to reward ourselves for all we've done for our kids' playdates is entertainment for us. Yes, our own playdate.

We could gather our friends and plan something fun. Why not tap into all the creativity we fostered in our youth when we had to figure out, on our own, how to keep ourselves busy. So let's call up all our friends who have proven to be true keepers over the years. Maybe organize a scavenger hunt around town. News of our plan will spread like wildfire. Think of the review we'll get. Even an ugly sweater party would be fun.

Throw their coats on the couch and *hope* they bring some alcohol. Remember, it's the snacks they will talk about on the ride home, so by all means nail it. And if the thought of scavenger hunts and parties overwhelms, no need to sit home bored. Go with the one-on-one scenario. Plan a date night for just the two of you, with *no* worries, Either way, it's going to be a breeze, as our kids' are off playing and dating on their own now.

It's time to reward ourselves with our own well-deserved time to play. Go enjoy!

And do it...

***amazingly* Guiltless!**

Chapter Eleven
College Cringes

Before we know it, we are cringing about the thought of sending our kids off to college. Thankfully, nature is very clever about this, and prepares us without our even knowing. Kids naturally become irritating as they prepare to leave home for the first time. Even kids who were easy through their high school years will develop some sort of intolerable behavior as they approach departure. These behaviors varied, but they all seemed to lose their semblance of orderliness, even former neatniks. Clothes piled up on their bedroom floor. Were they dirty? Were they clean? Who knew?

Would their roommate in college put up with this? Especially since you made them check neat on the roommate-preference questionnaire. But it was nature's way of preparing child and parent to separate. And it worked! It was much easier to pack the car for a kid we were exasperated with.

Likewise, they were happier to jump in the car if they were fed up with our nagging.

A teen's complete lack of regard to their surroundings was evident by the loud crashing sound heard when they walked in the door. Running down the stairs, we would meet them halfway, as they nonchalantly lumbered up. "What in the world was that?" we asked, thinking it had to be a bookshelf falling off the wall. They returned a blank stare. Regaining composure, as well as our balance on the stairs, we move past them. And there it was, a day's worth of their life dropped in the middle of the kitchen, blocking all access routes. Cookie crumbs all over the counter, milk carton on the table, and the door wide open. You're furious, and they were barricaded in their room. Evidently the plan was for us to clean it all up. But on the counter next to the cookie crumbs, lies an envelope from their first-choice college. Flying back up the stairs with the envelope in hand, completely forgetting about the crime scene once called a kitchen, we knock wildly on the barricaded door. They opened the letter and it was confirmed, they'd been accepted. You can hardly believe it as they wrote the essay for the application during a twenty-minute car ride home from the dentist and sent it out two minutes before the deadline. But we made it, oh right, they made it!

Parents will always remember where they were and what they were doing when they got the news of those first acceptance letters. In one case, I was in a store buying Easter candy when I got the call. Keeping my voice steady on the phone took everything I had. After hanging up, I slipped behind the display of orange-foiled chocolate carrots to hide the tears streaming down my face. How can human emotions accommodate exuberance, panic, and heartbreak simultaneously? But they do.

From then on, everything changed. Reality struck. The college-bound child is leaving home. Every waking minute became about them, and even some sleeping ones. We doted on them like royalty as we ceremonially made our way to all senior "lasts." You know, the last sporting event, last concert, last open house, last awards banquet. All of which required taking pictures, a sentimental lump in the throat, sometimes a flower or balloon, and always an extra-late curfew. We congratulated them after each event and told them how proud we were of them, over and over and over again. It all fed into the life of privilege they acquired by becoming a high school senior. In a nutshell, the world revolved around them.

At some point we regained our sanity and got back in touch with our inner parent. The one with a firm handle on the enough-is-enough model of parenting. Often the college-bound child's siblings snapped us out of it. They too got tired of stepping over the royal highness's crap in the kitchen and pointed out they'd like to see *their* favorite dinner on the table once in a while. So between that and the inevitable straw that broke the camel's back, we surfaced from the high school senior spell. Those straws were funny. They came with no warning whatsoever. For us, it was the smirk on the face of our senior sitting in the front row of the last National Honor Society ceremony. What a little thing, a straw, but my husband and I looked at each other that night and after taking the mandatory picture, and dropping a sentimental tear, we kicked into action...because enough was enough. We approached our child, who was waiting for his twenty-fifth congratulation of the month, escorted him to the car, and reamed him out the whole way home. He had forgotten we were his parents and not members of his royal court. This was a defining moment in preparing him to leave the nest, as he now wanted to go more than ever.

So we helped him pack, or we packed, the $2,000.00 of life essentials we bought for him over the summer to begin his life as a college student. Thank goodness someone bought the collapsible hamper as a graduation gift. The van looked like the sides would burst and off you went. Taking our kids to college was both physically and emotionally exhausting. Physically, because colleges seemed to think we were camels and we could traipse up three flights of stairs multiple times carrying microwaves, TVs, and other large items. Do we loft the bed or not? Let's try it both ways. Once sitting on the front steps, dripping in perspiration, thinking you're finally finished, a passing parent carrying a mini fridge mentioned going to the opposite side of campus to get an ID card. You wondered why they knew that and you didn't.

Worn out with the move-in, we then had to muster up energy to handle the emotions involved with leaving him to survive on his own for the first time in his life. Mothers seem to handle this by insisting on making their kid's bed; fathers by slapping a twenty in their palm. Let's face it, we're never really sure they can do this.

How about meeting the roommates? The people our child would be living with, shoulder to shoulder, for the entire year. Close parental scrutinizing of the roommate was unavoidable. That first impression was all about their reaction to Dad's bringing-everything-but-the-kitchen-sink joke. A blank stare, not even cracking a smile was reason for concern. "That kid has the personality of a doorknob," I whispered while assembling a shoe holder and made a mental note to check the handbook's section on switching roommates.

Luckily, the resident assistant showed up. I remember looking at the RA with such relief. *Oh good, someone in charge who's going to look after my child. Maybe they'll even be helpful with the roommate situation.* They smiled and chuckled at the kitchen-sink joke and seemed genuinely interested in our kid. They asked all the right questions and answered an enthusiastic yes to knowing Heimlich and CPR. They even offer information about all the parent presentations you're certain your kid didn't mention. Unfortunately, as time went by, we learned the RA was a college-arranged moving-day prop, never to be seen or heard from again.

Then it was off to buy another hundred dollars' worth of hooks and organizers and the "last" lunch. Kids like to make this quick because they have been texting friends they met at orientation all day and can't wait to meet up. At that point, your best chance of going to a parent presentation, or even the convocation ceremony was your being from out of town. Even then our kids would try to get the good-bye out of the way, hopefully without a fuss...well that's easier said than done.

To walk away knowing we're not going to see them every day or even hear their voice, is very hard. Will they call? Do I now have to depend on texting, or even worse, make a Facebook? Maybe Skype will be the answer. On and on the turmoil goes until it's actually time to say good-bye. My technique for this was sunglasses, regardless of the weather, because you cry. Most of the way home you cry. You occasionally calmed down, regrouped then cried again. If you didn't cry, you developed acute perforating ulcers from holding in the cry.

Each August, all over the country, parents cry their eyes out while driving home from leaving their kids at college for the first time. They wonder what their child is doing that night.

Worrying about what they are going to have for dinner. Was the crash course on laundry enough? Once again, can they really do this?

Before long, parents' weekend rolled around. That first visit back to their dorm room stays embedded in a parent's memory forever. Of course, what did we expect, that they would consider us company and spend the day prepping? I remember walking in and immediately starting to fold clothes and organize the shoes strewn all over the place. The serious roommate gave me another one of those glares, but this time I glared right back. How could they live like that? No wonder they required a meningitis vaccine before entering college. Better grab the hand sanitizer out of the car and leave it on their desk...after using it. Things improved once out of the room. They seemed glad to see us, even if it's because of the nice meal they were about to be taken out for and another twenty Dad would surely slip them.

Regardless, it was good to see them dressed in what you assumed were clean clothes. Well-nourished from what you assumed was a well-balanced meal plan. And generally happy from what you assumed was success in their classes. In reality, they hadn't done laundry for two weeks and were wearing their underwear inside out. They'd had nothing but pizza and burgers since they arrived, and they slept through six out of ten of their 8:00 a.m. classes.

We didn't need to know this, didn't want to know this, so we didn't know this, until long after they graduate. That's if they stuck with the five-year-statute-of-limitation rule on telling us things. Leaving them after this visit was much easier after seeing firsthand they'd somehow figured out how to survive without us. They assured us they liked it and established the roommate was fine, just hungover...which was somehow supposed to be reassuring.

Drinking in college was always a worry before kids reached the legal age. During tours, the student guides confidently assured us, while somehow walking backwards, that the campus was "dry." As we followed them in a herd, hanging on every word, we'd nod with satisfaction. Funny how there was not a student to be found during the 9:00 a.m. tour, and when we left at noon, the students who emerged sure didn't look like they were playing Scrabble all night. A protective sense of denial kicked in at that point. It wasn't until our daughter came home and wanted to bring back Gatorade to help alleviate hangovers that reality hit. Even after this realization, we had no choice but to close a "dry" eye to it, and hope for the best.

Another thing I chose to close my eyes to was all the travel abroad options, giving our kids the impression they were entitled to see the world as part of their college experience. This was, of course, on top of extraordinarily high tuition and astonishingly low financial-aid packages. I don't blame the kids. The universities presented these opportunities as if they would make or break their future. Did they get a commission on the number of kids they sent off on world tours? I could see the benefit of experiencing another culture for some majors, but for all of them?

Take occupational therapy for instance. We told our daughter the muscles and tendons of Europeans are no different than those of Americans. The problem was, even when we were dead set on putting the kibosh on this, we could be tricked. Our son's architecture department disguised a semester in the Dominican Republic as an independent study course. They painted a picture of him working on a special project there, the opportunity of a lifetime. It started out no more expensive than a regular semester, but, like everything else in college, the price tag grew once we'd signed him up. It was frightening having him so far away in a third-world country, but we relaxed once hearing he was staying across the street from a five-star resort and frequenting their restaurant for dinner.

Later we also learned this *opportunity of a lifetime* included quite a bit of kayaking, snorkeling, and salsa dancing.

You win some you lose some.

Anyway, wasn't it enough having to hear

about the regular weekend goings on, which evidently started on Thirsty Thursday? We innocently called to see how they were doing, and they informed us they were on their way out to party in the city. After a hard, audible gulp, you asked how they could get into clubs when they weren't of legal drinking age. After they stopped laughing, they announced there are underage clubs that didn't serve alcohol. Somehow that sounded like the backward-walking student tour guide. Someone by the name of Boozy was driving, and they *might* crash at *someone's* place. So we stayed up all night worrying, and the next day when they didn't answer their phone because they forgot to charge it, we resisted the urge to call the police. Besides, what would we have said to them, "My kid *might* have crashed at *someone's* house after partying at an underage club in the city? When we finally reached them, once their phone charged, they couldn't understand our dismay. Meanwhile they sounded like they'd been up all night because they had been, and they explained how this was all just part of the college experience. Our patience dissolved as we attempted to discuss the risks involved in their weekend adventures.

Suddenly their reception was bad. "You're breaking up. I'll call you later," and the phone went dead. It didn't even matter, because they were safe, and that was all we really wanted to know. Although keeping their phone charged would have been nice, too.

It was also nice when our kids considered the array of interesting elective courses available as a way to broaden their college experience. That's if they could keep in perspective the courses were intended to broaden, not change their path. In an effort to branch out by taking an elective geology course, our one son decided to switch his major. The next semester he wanted to change it to sociology then English, poetry, and finally economics. He lost sight of the goal in the game, which was...get a career. Trying to help them out by pointing out their strengths was useless. After all parents could not be trusted to make such a judgment call.

Our job then switched to making their visits home as pleasant as possible. So, from the minute they walk in the door and appear from behind their laundry hamper, we were on. It was like "Johnny Comes Marching Home." The aroma of their favorite meal filled the air as their spotless bedroom awaited. The cupboards were stocked with their favorite snacks and their loving parents have cleared the calendar for the weekend. Yup, back to the royal treatment. The siblings only agreed because it's temporary. The college students settled in as if they'd never left, enjoyed their favorite meal, and talked excitedly about all they've done. It was our opportunity to use our keen parental investigative skills to see how they really were doing. We hung on every word to detect any suspicion of a potential problem. Then, back out the door they went to hang out with friends. Next morning, over a nice breakfast, we talked a little more, and back out the door they went. They swung by for another dinner before returning to school with a laundry basket full of clean clothes...yup, washed and folded for them. Thing is, we didn't even complain about this because we got a dose of them...all we needed to be satisfied they were doing okay.

After four years of this, it was no surprise that graduation was our favorite part of the college experience. Done with the packing, unpacking, moving them in, moving them out, and calls to send money. Time to celebrate! Until our student announces they don't want to go to the commencement ceremony.

"Why don't you want to go?" we asked with desperation.

"It's stupid," they responded.

"How could you not want to celebrate all your hard work?"

"Stupid, no one else is going."

As instructed, we'd booked a hotel room six months in advance, so someone must have been going, and war had been declared. A parent's first line of attack is always the disappointed card. The kid retaliated with an it's-about-me card, and therefore it should be their choice.

Second round, you threw out the you'll-regret-it card. They retaliated with the denial card.

It was time to pull out the heavy artillery. You hated to go there but what choice remained? So out came the money card. They couldn't beat the money card. The only part about their being flat broke by the end of college that worked to our advantage. You threatened to squash the gravy train, they were paralyzed, at our mercy, and off to commencement we went. Winning this battle was our first reward for making it through the college years. Never feel guilty, we deserved it. They did, too, they just didn't realize it yet. It will be one of those things they will look back on, and be glad they did. So we should be glad we stood strong, persevered, and, yes, pulled the money card in the end.

Our true reward for making it through our kid's college years was not immediate. It took a little while for them to get on their financial feet. If they came back home after graduation it could, in fact, felt like the whole plan backfired. So many years of effort, and they are back where they started. Parents were still paying many of their bills, feeding them, housing them, and, yes, stepping over their stuff. But we shouldn't despair. True rewards were just around the corner with our child's complete financial independence! Before we knew it, their career took off, and a college grad was paying their own way through life.

Finally all their, and our, hard work had paid off, and the bills started arriving with *their* name on them. They now get placed in a nice, neat pile for *them* to pick up each week. Oh, how we stand back and beam with pride at the rewards of this magnificent accomplishment!

And do it...

amazingly **Guiltless!**

Chapter Twelve
They're Back

A kid returning home after college is one of those things in life deserving of a special term. I don't know who came up with it, but they nailed it perfectly with the expression boomerangers. We throw them out into the college world, they twirl round and round, and then end up right back in our hands. As they land, it seems like both a forever ago and a split second ago that we tossed them out into the world. How can that be? Maybe it's the whirlwind of thrills and spills both they, and we, as their parents undergo during their flight. Regardless, they're back and this becomes another parental experience we completely underestimate.

Our kids going off to college is their first opportunity to strike out on their own. It's their time to *accomplish their goals, conquer the world*, all those salutations mentioned in their graduation cards way back when they began. If there was a third page to those graduation cards it would read, *Until you graduate, are out of money, and have to move back home to get on your feet.* Funny how we never considered the possibility when we sent them off. Instead, we were devastated our child was leaving us, and set up the shrine in their bedroom. Maybe that explains our shock when they called with their after-graduation plan.

"You've decided to come home after graduation? Oh, well, of course it's okay, honey." Niceties, niceties, love ya, bye...gulp. Okay, sure, of course, that makes perfect sense. The room was empty, well, except for the treadmill and office we set up, but we can move them. Yes, it will be nice to have them back home with us again...another gulp.

And it was nice. The first couple of weeks when it was all brand new and we were operating like the perfect hosts and they were operating like the perfect guest, it was very nice. Just like their visits home, we made all their favorite meals and even threw in a little laundry for them. Likewise, they were thrilled to be fussed over again. The problems began when they assumed it was going to continue. Eventually, we remembered that this is the same kid we raised for twenty-one years, our own flesh and blood, not a guest. Our house taking on the look of a college dorm reinforced the need to end the host/guest relationship, as their stuff was all over the place. Keys on the kitchen counter, shoes in the middle of the family room, a computer on the couch, glasses and bowls on the coffee table, something on every flat surface. Oh, wait, non-flat surfaces, too. I forgot about the clothes draped over the banister, back of kitchen chairs, and the arms of the couch. Also, my pet peeve of wet towels on the floor...again!

Would they have dried their wet bodies with a throw rug everyone'd stepped on? So basically, we have to pull the throw rug out from under them.

Let's face it, we'd gotten accustomed to having control over our environment. Things had pretty much stayed where we put them while they were gone. We forgot the kind of disarray we lived with all the years we were raising them and developed a new sort of existence, a sensible one! So we started to reel them in. This rarely goes well. We nicely asked them to pick up their stuff, easing them into the realization the jig is up. Their favorite response became, "I've got it."

When we asked, "Can you clean up your breakfast dishes?" they responded,

"I've got it."

"When are you getting your six pairs of shoes out of the doorway?"

"I've got it."

"Could you throw out the moldy pizza crust in your room today?"

An annoyed, "I've got it."

Problem is, they didn't "got it." Now we're irritated and they couldn't understand why. "What are you getting so worked up about?" they ask. They simply could not comprehend our issues, when they had done us the favor of coming back home to live.

At times, we wondered if we were the ones

being unreasonable. Yes, our boomerangers had us doubting ourselves. We wondered why we couldn't ignore it like we used to when they were growing up and the house was always in disarray. Had we become too set in our ways? Did we have unreasonable expectations? We may even be experiencing guilt! Oh, thank goodness I'm writing this book. Hopefully these fleeting thoughts quickly vanished when reality set in, they came back to us unable to pick up a single, solitary thing.

Besides, wasn't it a big enough challenge to survive without our evening couch naps? These became a necessary part of our daily-sleep requirement, and got completely disrupted with their return. The kids got to the TV first every evening, leaving us wandering around the house doing this and that until bedtime. When we finally crawled up the stairs to bed, our boomerangers were heading out the door to begin their evening activities.

"Where are you going at this hour?" we asked, with a tone of surprised concern. They reminded us they have been on their own for a while, and have not had to account to anybody for their whereabouts. OooKaay. Without our couch nap we were too tired to process this before they're out the door on their unaccounted-for way, leaving us wondering if this issue trumps leaving their junk around. The problem is, no matter how tired we were when our heads hit the pillow, there was no avoiding listening for the garage door, signaling they're home safe. Yes, eyes were closed, but a portion of our brain stayed awake, making it impossible to enter the all-important REM cycle of sleep.

Much like we did when they were babies, sleeping with one ear open, but we were twenty-five years younger then. This lack of real sleep at our age messes with our psyche. So when we were peering at the alarm clock at 1:00 am with still no sign of them, our mind went crazy with possibilities of why they were not home yet. And if we tried to explain this to them they called it another ridiculous, unnecessary thing we do. We needed to "relax," which becomes another one of their favorite responses. Not until they're the ones listening for the garage door and peering at the clock waiting for their own kids will they understand!

It was also hard for them to understand your having the nerve to charge them room and board. A little something to get them accustomed to being a part of the real world. It barely covered the food, water, heat, toilet paper, shampoo, soap, and the electric bill from their constantly running electronics, but it was a contribution. Thing is, asking our kids for money is never easy. It goes against our parental instinct to care for them. We try to counter the emotion by assuring ourselves we are cultivating responsibility. It's good for them, but, of course, they'll never see it that way. They saw it as their parents taking them to the cleaners. Remember, they still thought they had given us this golden opportunity to live with them again. Once they recovered from the shock, it was usually necessary to clarify what room and board includes. For instance, our beer, wine, and hard liquor were not included, even if they offered to replace it. Actually, especially if they offered to replace it, because they can only afford screw-top wines and below-bottom-shelf liquor. Protein powder drinks, an organic diet, and tropical fruits for$4.00 each, also not included. No wonder they ran out of spending money so often when they were on their own. I refused to relax on this.

It gets confusing for kids when they come back home and we start to make demands on them. They're used to doing what they want, when they want, how they want.

That's why asking them to pitch in with chores on top of paying room and board really throws them for a loop. They expected their rent to include this. Sharing the workload was another attempt to get them accustomed to the real world.

Usually, our idea of this and their idea of it, were two completely different things. Our boomerangers thought doing their part was moving their shoes from in front of the door and putting their glass in the sink after you ask them three times. So when you dropped the bomb you'd like them to empty the dishwasher every day or take out the garbage, they were flabbergasted. When you threw in lawn mowing and snow removal, they needed resuscitated. Some parents try waiting for an offer from their boomerangers to take on a few of the routine chores...ha ha, delusional. It's much better to be direct about this and ask them right out, "Would you take out the garbage every night for us?" The "for us" is just for effect. We all know they could care less if the garbage goes out. Sometimes, we followed it with a, "Would you mind?"

That's a nicety parents frequently use but never really mean. We knew before asking they would mind. They were back to "Yeah, yeah, I got it." Tone definitely irritated, with a touch of insult. Okay, we expected that but were proud we took a stand. Until it didn't get done. We swore we wouldn't do it for them, but could only put it off for so long. Completely out of clean glasses, and smelling the kitchen garbage in our bedroom, we did it...but, just one more time!

Enough is enough, we argued in our heads; they cannot keep getting away with this. We find ourselves planning out the best time to address it.

Obviously early morning was out of the question for discussing anything with twenty-year-olds. Walking in the door right after work was also out, leaving the small window between dinner time and early evening before they were out the door again. I usually kept my options open on this, working within the variables. Weighing the right mood vs. the right barometric pressure vs. my horoscope. When the time seemed right I started with a nice, calm lighthearted mention of the ignored chore, exploring the possibility of it being fit into the evening's agenda. I tried not to sound sarcastic and even interject a little humor when I could. Now if the chore still didn't get done, they'd entered very shaky territory. I then reminded, which led to begging, which led to a pitiful plea, which always, always led to anger. Yup, I laid em out! Trying not to scare the neighbors, but indeed letting them have it. How could we possibly expect to have any patience left? It's not like we were asking them to polish the silver or roof the house. So as we took out the garbage, just one more time, after they ran out the door apologizing and promising to do it later, we at least knew in our hearts we had set them straight. End of discussion...gulp.

There was also the tendency to become our kids' personal secretaries when they moved back home.

"Mom, can you make me a hair appointment?"

"Dad, can you set me up for an oil change at the garage you use?"

Can you mail this, can you fax this, would you make a copy of this, on and on it goes. I call this the twenty-year-old go away, go away, help, help syndrome. Our tendency is to make this work for them. That darned old instinct again. This part of parenting takes a non-parenting approach, where we really have to shut off our natural parenting instincts. Don't worry, I have never met a parent who was able to do this for any length of time.

Better to put our efforts toward the challenge of meal planning. Were they coming home for dinner or not? Make four pork chops or six? Their plans changed at a moment's notice. As we're sitting there enjoying steak for two, they'd come rolling in the door, and we were salvaging a plate for them. How can we not feed our kid? Or we'd made enough for them, and ended up staring at it because they decided to meet a friend. We didn't dare throw out the plastic containers from the Italian takeout place anymore and started to feel like we worked for Meals On Wheels, packaging food to be eaten at a later date. Even when they didn't show up for dinner, the saved meal got eaten when they walked in the door at midnight, evident by the Italian food containers left sitting on the counter.

Couldn't colleges help us out with this? How about a nice mandatory course in Expectations of Moving Back Home 101. Why hasn't anyone thought of this? First lecture could be "How to turn *off* lights." Evidently kids never have to turn off the lights in a dorm or college apartment. I thought this was the generation focused on energy conservation. When you add the lights to the electronics they keep plugged in all night, the meter was really spinning. Honestly, I didn't know what half the cords in the family room went to. Again, a sigh of dismay when pointing out the soaring electric bill.

How about another lecture with the catchy title Job Interviews: Give Your Parents a Break. Because when we asked them if their resume is updated for their interview the next week, we got a nonchalant, "I will." Then we watched them print off their hopefully updated resume ten minutes before walking out the door. We held our breath that the printer didn't run out of ink, but they didn't seem worried at all.

When we asked them if they had everything they need for their interview next week, we got another nonchalant, "Yup, I do." Then we watched them put on an outfit that's been on their bed all week, grab a pen from the kitchen counter and the tablet next to the phone, again on their way out the door. And when we asked if they knew where they were going for their interview next week, we got a nonchalant, "I'll use my GPS." Then we watch them punch the address into their GPS as they were about to leave. Of course, we would have prepared days in advance and when we voiced that suggestion, they delivered a lecture on how uptight we are and how we, again, need to relax. So we figured we'd just let them learn the hard way. Experience is the best teacher. But somehow, for some unknown reason, they end up getting the job. How? They've done everything they weren't supposed to do in preparing for it. Maybe we really *do* need to relax. Again, they have us doubting ourselves.

No doubt, a lecture titled Real World Time wouldn't hurt, either. My daughter asked me to book her an eye exam, secretarial work again, and stated, while flipping her hair back, "Sunday works best for me."

My son headed off to the mall one week night at 9:00 p.m. and was furious it was closed. Neither of them could understand why the public library closed at 8:00 p.m. Breakfast, lunch, and dinner were on complete flex time for them and varied daily.

Completely exasperated with the hours of the dining hall at home, they accuse us of making them show up for the senior citizen early-bird special. They wanted us to watch a movie with them at nine o'clock on a week night, and wanted to start their laundry at ten. They had our heads spinning as we tried to remember what's reasonable, and we even started to consider the idea of giving a weeknight movie a try. Yup, again, doubting ourselves.

Some of this stems from the fact that when our kids boomerang back to us, they let one foot in the door but leave the other foot out. In their minds they never really entirely move back home. This may account for their inability to conform to our way of life, which used to be their way of life, but that doesn't seem to matter. They think it's just a temporary living arrangement until something better comes up or, rather they're hoping. Sometimes the something better does come up fairly quickly, and sometimes we have to give it a little help. You know, make the grass on the other side of the fence look greener. We simply have to keep to our expectations and not worry about making them too happy. This is nothing new, as parents have been using this technique with their children for generations. It started way back in the Stone Age when a young adult became disgruntled when asked to chisel out a new set of eating utensils for the family. Exasperated with his parents, he moved into his own little cave. Eating salamanders to afford it, but he was happy because he was on his own. Same thing happens now, but instead of salamanders it's ramen noodles.

All we had to do is keep to our course of real-world expectations, and before we knew it we'd be packing up our old dishes and tucking our boomeranger into a nice, little place of their own.

Of course, when it did finally happen it takes

some switching gears and it was hard to avoid the self-doubt. Did we push them out? Should we have given them more time to get on their feet? Come on, even the parenting books agree with our chickadees leaving the nest and reassure us on our quickly finding our rhythm again. The feat of our boomerangers striking out on their own has even been given its own well-deserved term...Independence Day!

When a kid reaches the monumental milestone of Independence Day, it is a defining moment in the life of a parent. We will eventually get to the point where we will even stop buying them socks and underwear. For some reason that is the hardest thing to let go of. I have to admit, I am still guilty of throwing socks in the Christmas stockings. Regardless, our lives will revert back to being an Empty Nester. Our electric bills will fall back down below our mortgage payment. We will no longer be woken at 2:00 a.m. by a rustling in the kitchen of leftovers being warmed, and even our sleep patterns will return. Our boomerangers have declared their independence and we can now refocus on ourselves. No looking back, on to an amazing life with us as the nucleus, and our kids as the circling electrons. Basically, it's simple science.

Parenting is the most important thing we will ever do in our lifetime. No matter how accomplished we are, or how many recognitions we've earned, nothing will ever have as much importance in our lives as our role of parenting. We have tapped into every fiber of our being to raise our children, parts we didn't know existed. When it felt impossible, we dug deep and found a way. When they thrilled us, it was a level of joy we never realized we could feel. Nothing will ever compare. This book has reminded us of all that went into this amazing endeavor, and why it's finally time to reward ourselves. We have recognized the accomplishment. We will savor the accomplishment. And most importantly, we will now reward ourselves for the accomplishment!

And do it...

amazingly Guiltless!

About the Author

Diane Stolz was born and bred in Pittsburgh, PA, home of six time Super Bowl Champs! She left her Italian family there and moved to Connecticut when she and Tom married, but she will always be a Steeler fan. They began the venture of raising kids in 1985 with the birth of their first child. With two more to follow, they were swallowed up into the world of parenting and have not come up for air until now. Now that they have become...Empty Nesters!

Diane has written throughout her life. She loves stitching words together to create a piece of work. Now that she is an Empty Nester, with actual time to herself, she can indulge. With outstanding material for her first book just handed to her...Raising kids!

CPSIA information can be obtained at www.ICGtesting.com
Printed in the USA
LVOW01s1326030915

452702LV00024B/588/P